NEW TEST

Gen

A.T. Lincoln

2 CORINTHIANS

2 CORINTHIANS

Larry Kreitzer

Sheffield Academic Press

For Dave

κοινωνὸς ἐμός

(2 Cor. 8.23)

From that first fateful day in our high school English literature class (when we were assigned a common desk based on the alphabetical closeness of our names) until now, he has been a fellow traveller on the pathway of faith despite all the twists and turns we have each encountered in the road. I am privileged to own him as my friend, and fortunate to be claimed as such by him.

Published by Sheffield Academic Press Ltd
Mansion House
19 Kingfield Road
Sheffield S11 9AS
England
www.SheffieldAcademicPress.com

Printed on acid-free paper in Great Britain by
Biddles Ltd
Guildford, Surrey

British Library Cataloguing in Publication Data

A catalogue record for this book is available
from the British Library

ISBN 1-85075-789-5

Contents

Preface

It is commonly remarked that in 2 Corinthians Paul is at his most self-revealing. This is true enough, but paradoxically 2 Corinthians is also the place where Paul is at his most enigmatic. To attempt an interpretation of the letter is to enter a hermeneutical minefield; a host of interlocking problems face the reader from the outset and it is difficult to find any place where a single step may be safely taken. It seems as if every assumption one makes about the nature of the letter, as well as the ideas and events recorded within it (or is it *them?*), is open to serious question from any number of directions. So many of the exegetical decisions that one makes when trying to understand the meaning of a given text are absolutely at the mercy of a host of other decisions which have to be made about other key texts; and it comes as no surprise to discover that the interpreter of each of those texts is often in search of some degree of assurance, some fixed point of certainty, by looking over his or her shoulder at the passage with which one is wrestling. 2 Corinthians quickly becomes a complex web of interconnected problems which tax the ability of anyone to fathom them completely. If ever there was a claim for a New Testament document being described as 'the Gordian knot' of scholarship, it is 2 Corinthians! Yet a critical study of the epistle offers an immense number of opportunities, for some of the issues raised by the letter lie at the heart not only of Pauline thought but of New Testament scholarship generally.

For the past few years some brave and courageous students have ventured to 'walk the minefield' with me by attending my lectures on 'The Corinthian Correspondence' within the University of Oxford. My sincere hope is that this introduction to the epistle will serve as a means for a wider readership to engage this most challenging of Paul's letters.

LJK
Trinity Term 1995
Oxford

Abbreviations

AB	Anchor Bible Commentaries
ABD	Anchor Bible Dictionary
ABR	*Australian Biblical Review*
AC	Augsburg New Testament Commentary
AnBib	Analecta biblica
BBB	Bonner biblische Beiträge
BBC	Broadman Bible Commentary
BFT	Biblical Foundations in Theology
BHT	Beiträge zur historischen Theologie
BJRL	*Bulletin of the John Rylands University Library of Manchester*
BNTC	Black's New Testament Commentaries
BST	The Bible Speaks Today
BT	*The Bible Translator*
BTB	*Biblical Theology Bulletin*
BZNW	Beihefte zur ZNW
CBC	Cambridge Bible Commentaries
CBQ	*Catholic Biblical Quarterly*
CTM	*Concordia Theological Monthly*
EBC	Expositor's Bible Commentary
EC	Epworth Commentaries
EFN	Estudios de Filología Neotestamentaria
EGT	Expositor's Greek Testament
EvQ	*Evangelical Quarterly*
ExpTim	*Expository Times*
GNS	Good News Studies
HTR	*Harvard Theological Review*
IC	Interpretation Commentaries
ICC	International Critical Commentary
IDB	Interpreter's Dictionary of the Bible
JAAR	*Journal of the American Academy of Religion*
JBL	*Journal of Biblical Literature*
JJS	*Journal of Jewish Studies*
JRelS	*Journal of Religious Studies*
JSNT	*Journal for the Study of the New Testament*

JSNTSup	*Journal for the Study of the New Testament, Supplement Series*
JTS	*Journal of Theological Studies*
KPG	Knox Preaching Guides
MeyerK	H.A.W. Meyer (ed.), Kritisch-exegetischer Kommentar über das Neue Testament
MNTC	Moffatt New Testament Commentaries
NCB	New Century Bible
NICNT	New International Commentary on the New Testament
NIDNTT	C. Brown (ed.), *The New International Dictionary of New Testament Theology*
NovT	*Novum Testamentum*
NovTSup	*Novum Testamentum*, Supplements
NTTS	New Testament Theology Series
RB	*Revue Biblique*
SBEC	Studies in the Bible and Early Christianity
SBLSS	Society of Biblical Literature Semeia Series
SBT	Studies in Biblical Theology
SCJ	Studies in Christianity and Judaism
SE	*Studia Evangelica*
SJ	Studies in Judaism
SJT	*Scottish Journal of Theology*
SNTSMS	Society for New Testament Studies Monograph Series
TBC	Torch Biblical Commentaries
TNTC	Tyndale New Testament Commentaries
TS	*Theological Studies*
TynBul	*Tyndale Bulletin*
WBC	Word Biblical Commentary
WUNT	Wissenschaftliche Untersuchungen zum Neuen Testament
ZNW	*Zeitschrift für die neutestamentliche Wissenshcaft*

Suggestions for Reading

Fortunately, 2 Corinthians has been well served by English language commentaries in recent years, with the appearance of commentaries by V.P. Furnish (1984) and R.P. Martin (1986) being especially noteworthy, although the volume by Colin Kruse (1987) is a competent and readable alternative to these two contenders for the heavy-weight crown. Moreover, a fresh challenger is looming on the horizon as the forthcoming effort by M.E. Thrall (the first volume of which appeared in the summer of 1994) looks as if it will once again place 2 Corinthians at the centre of Pauline discussion and debate. The volumes by D. Carson (1984), P. Barnett (1988), F.W. Danker (1989) and N. Watson (1993) will also prove immensely valuable for those seeking a more accessible way into the Pauline letter, while the contribution by E. Best (1987) is a fine resource for the preacher or teacher who wants to tackle 2 Corinthians without being caught up in all the minutiae of technical detail. Taken together all of these commentaries provide ample food for thought on this most fascinating of the epistles of Paul. Several good introductions to Paul's life and thought are also available, including those by G. Bornkamm (1971), F.F. Bruce (1977), E.P. Sanders (1991), J. Ziesler (1990), and C.K. Barrett (1994). Finally, mention should also be made of the recently published *Dictionary of Paul and his Letters*, edited by G.F. Hawthorne, R.P. Martin and D.G. Reid (1993), which is an indispensable tool for those who want to engage in Pauline study and have a readable and up-to-date guide to critical scholarship by their side. Full details of all of these works, and many other monographs and articles useful for a study of 2 Corinthians, are available in the bibliography included at the end of the volume. In addition, secondary sources relating to specific topics discussed within the various chapters can be found at the conclusion of the chapter concerned.

1

PAUL AND THE FOUNDING
OF THE CHURCH AT CORINTH

One of the most important factors in the evaluation of Paul's
epistles to the church in Corinth is due consideration of the
city's history and social makeup. First-century Corinth was
above all a Roman city, the administrative capital of the
province of Achaia, ordered rebuilt by Julius Caesar shortly
before his assassination in 44 BCE. The area was dominated
by the Acrocorinth, which rises some 600 metres above the
surrounding plain and was the site of a temple dedicated to
Aphrodite. From this site a commanding view is afforded of
both the Gulf of Corinth and the Aegean Sea. The city itself
was strategically located in the Isthmus of Corinth on the all-
important trade route between Asia Minor and Italy. The
Emperor Nero (54–68 CE) is known to have attempted to cut
a canal through the narrow isthmus in order to facilitate
trade and save ships the long journey around the
Peloponnesus. Unfortunately the project was abandoned at
Nero's death and it was not until modern times, in 1893, that
a successful channel was constructed.

It is frequently noted that the ancient city was a rich
commercial centre, with a wide range of religious and
cultural beliefs in evidence, and that its character as a port
city, with harbours in Lechaeum on the west and Cenchreae
on the east, gave it something of a dubious moral reputation.
It was a city abounding in temples where cultic prostitution
was practised (cf. 1 Cor. 6.9-20 and 2 Cor. 12.20-21!), and the
moral laxity of the city lent itself to the creation of a Greek

verb (κορινθιάζεσθαι) denoting sexual license.

Corinth was closely associated in the ancient world with the Isthmian Games, which were second only to the Olympic and Pythian games in terms of importance. These Isthmian Games were held every two years outside the city and may help explain the athletic imagery Paul uses in 1 Cor. 9.24-27. It has been suggested that the presence of the games was what attracted Paul to Corinth in the first place and was the reason why he made the city his base of operations in Greece.

In short, there is every indication that the city of Corinth was a cultural and religious crossroads of the first century CE. This may help to explain something of the party factionalism characterizing the Christian congregation which sprang up there and which occasioned Paul's letters to the believers there. The passage in 1 Cor. 1.10-12 which describes the various groups at work within the church is crucial to any attempt at reconstructing the problems Paul attempts to put right, although there is no consensus as to who the opponents Paul engages were. Neither is it clear precisely what the relationship was between the opponents in 1 Corinthians and the opponents in 2 Corinthians. This issue forms one of the greatest focal points in scholarly discussion of the Corinthian correspondence and will no doubt continue to do so for years to come.

Date and Founding of the Church at Corinth

It is generally acknowledged that Paul was instrumental in the founding of the church at Corinth while on his second missionary journey; that Silas and Timothy were co-workers with Paul in this endeavour also seems indicated (2 Cor. 1.19). Not only do we have the evidence of the Corinthian epistles themselves for this, but we find that the contact between Paul and Corinth is discussed in Acts 18.1-18. These verses are extremely important in establishing the chronology of Paul's various missionary journeys, especially since they contain not only a reference to the expulsion of the Jews from Rome by the Emperor Claudius (mentioned in 18.2), but an explicit reference to the proconsulship of Gallio (mentioned in 18.12). Most scholars agree that the expulsion of the Jews from Rome is probably to be associated with the event recorded in Suetonius's *Claudius* 25.4 and thus dated to 49 CE. The discovery of a number of fragments of an inscription in Delphi in 1905 provided confirmation of the position of Gallio (brother of the famous philosopher Seneca) and allows his proconsulship to be fairly accurately dated. On the basis of this epigraphic evidence (now consisting of some nine fragments) Gallio is generally acknowledged to have held the office of proconsul of the province of Achaia in 51–52 CE, a fact which provides us with one of the few historical certainties(?) against which to chart Paul's journeys. Thus, if we take the reference in Acts 18.11 to Paul having spent some eighteen months in Corinth to be accurate, we can plot this against Gallio's proconsulship and postulate that Paul was in Corinth from the autumn of 50 CE until the late spring of 52 CE when he undertook a journey to Jerusalem and Antioch (cf. Acts 18.18-23). Assuming that the encounter with Gallio recorded in 18.12-17 took place shortly after the new proconsul took office, and that it was designed to test Gallio's attitude towards Judaism, we may date Paul's appearance before the tribunal sometime between July and October of 51 CE.

Yet not everything is as straightforward as it might first appear; other possibilities of historical reconstruction exist. Occasionally it has been suggested from the composite nature of Acts 18.1-8 that in fact two separate visits by Paul to Corinth are conflated within these verses. The first visit is associated with the edict of Claudius and Paul's befriending of the exiled Jewish Christians Aquila and Priscilla (18.1-4); the second visit is associated with the arrival of Silas and Timothy from Macedonia (see 1 Thess. 3.6) when Paul's preaching ministry in the city leads to friction with the Jewish authorities and ultimately to the apostle's appearance before the tribunal. Generally those who pursue this interpretation of Paul's visits to Corinth date the edict of Claudius to 41 CE. Thus, an initial visit to Corinth in 41 CE is proposed, in addition to the subsequent visit made in 51–52 CE during the proconsulship of Gallio.

Corinth as a Metropolitan Centre for Paul's Ministry

Corinth is one of the places most intimately linked in the New Testament with Paul's apostolic ministry to the Gentiles, the other two major sites being Antioch and Ephesus. This has led to a view that Paul was predominantly a metropolitan man and that he concentrated his ministry within the great cities of the ancient world. More is known about the church of Corinth than about any other congregation associated with Paul's ministry, mainly through the correspondence the apostle directed there. By carefully combing through the Pauline corpus it is possible to identify the names of a dozen or so key people who in some way or another fall within the orbit of the church of Corinth, including Cephas, Timothy, Titus, Silas, Aquila and Priscilla, Apollos, Crispus, Stephanas, Gaius, Chloe, Erastus and Phoebe.

Paul's Fellow-Labourers at Corinth

Paul's friendship with Aquila and Priscilla (or Prisca, as Paul tends to refer to her) was apparently a deep and abiding one extending over many years. Paul mentions the pair, with whom he had worked as a tentmaker during the early days of the establishment of the church at Corinth, at several points in his letters. Thus we find that he communicates their greetings to the church in Corinth in 1 Cor. 16.19 (probably written from Ephesus in 53 or 54 CE) and sends warm greetings to them in Rom. 16.3-4, mentioning their willingness to risk their lives for him. It appears from Acts 18.24-27 that while in Ephesus both Aquila and Priscilla were influential in the Christian education of Apollos, a personality who invites a number of suggestive, if unprovable, hypotheses about the collection of the documents we now know as the New Testament. Not least is the suggestion, proposed by no less a figure than Martin Luther, that Apollos was the author of the anonymous epistle to the Hebrews. Apollos is described in Acts 18.27 as undertaking a mission to Achaia, and in Acts 19.1 he is noted as being in Corinth. That the eloquent young convert was an important figure in the life of the church at Corinth seems certain, although he appears at no time to have been anything other than a loyal supporter of Paul. Indeed, Paul lists Apollos as among those who were with him in Ephesus at the time that he composed 1 Corinthians (1 Cor. 16.12).

Paul the Tentmaker

Clearly Paul worked as a tentmaker in Corinth in order to support himself so that he could carry on his ministry as the 'apostle to the Gentiles'. The apostle hints at his independence in this regard in 1 Cor. 4.12, unashamedly declaring that he worked with his own hands (cf. 1 Thess. 2.9). One can also catch glimpses of Paul's pride in his self-sufficiency in 1 Cor. 9.18 where he proudly declares that he has preached the gospel to the Corinthians free of charge, and in 2 Cor. 11.9 and 12.13, where he boasts of the fact that he did not burden, and does not plan to burden, the church in his visits to them. Instead, he seems content to rely upon his own tentmaking skills and the generosity of Macedonian Christians to make ends meet (see 2 Cor. 11.8-9 and Phil. 4.5). This practice of self-support apparently resulted in some criticism of his apostolic ministry, and Paul defends his practice strongly in 2 Corinthians. For Paul, his lowly state—his having to work for a living—was a sign that he was a true servant of Christ and a genuine apostle; in the service of the gospel he boasts that he has worked harder than anyone else (2 Cor. 11.23). Furthermore, Paul alludes to the precariousness of his lifestyle, his financial poverty and homelessness in 2 Cor. 6.10. In 6.10 he describes himself as 'poor, yet making many rich', and in 8.9 he makes a similar statement about the Lord Jesus Christ himself, noting that 'though he was rich, yet for your sakes he became poor, so that by his poverty you might become rich'. The juxtaposition of these two statements probably indicates that Paul saw himself following in the tradition of Jesus by living the life of poverty and humility that he did. In short, there is much to be gleaned from a careful consideration of some of the nuances surrounding Paul's passing references to his life as a working-class man.

Suggestions for Further Reading

On the City of Corinth

W.A. Meeks, *The First Urban Christians: The Social World of the Apostle Paul* (London: Yale University Press, 1983).

J. Murphy-O'Connor, *St Paul's Corinth: Texts and Archaeology* (GNS, 6; Wilmington, DE: Michael Glazier, 1983).

—'Corinth', *ABD*, I, pp. 1134-39.

Paul the Tentmaker

P.W. Barnett, 'Tentmaking', in G.F. Hawthorne, R.P. Martin and D.G. Reid (eds.), *Dictionary of Paul and his Letters* (Leicester: Inter-Varsity Press, 1993), pp. 925-27.

R.F. Hock, 'Paul's Tentmaking and the Problem of his Social Class', *JBL* 97 (1978), pp. 555-64.

—'The Workshop as a Social Setting for Paul's Missionary Preaching', *CBQ* 41 (1979), pp. 438-50.

—*The Social Context of Paul's Ministry: Tentmaking and Apostleship* (Philadelphia: Fortress Press, 1980).

On Pauline Chronology

L.C.A. Alexander, 'Chronology of Paul', in G.F. Hawthorne, R.P. Martin and D.G. Reid (eds.), *Dictionary of Paul and his Letters* (Leicester: Inter-Varsity Press, 1993), pp. 115-23.

G.S. Duncan, *St. Paul's Ephesian Ministry* (London: Hodder & Stoughton, 1929).

C.J. Hemer, 'Observations on Pauline Chronology', in D.A. Hagner and M.J. Harris (eds.), *Pauline Studies: Essays Presented to F.F. Bruce on his 70th Birthday* (Exeter: Paternoster Press, 1980), pp. 3-18.

R. Jewett, *A Chronology of Paul's Life* (Philadelphia: Fortress Press, 1979).

J. Knox, *Chapters in a Life of Paul* (London: SCM Press, rev. edn, 1989).

—'Chapters in a Life of Paul—A Response to Robert Jewett and Gerd Luedemann', in B. Corley (ed.), *Colloquy on New Testament Studies: A Time for Reappraisal and Fresh Approaches* (Macon, GA: Mercer University Press, 1983), pp. 339-64.

G. Ogg, *The Chronology of the Life of Paul* (London: Epworth Press, 1968).

On the Relationship between the Pauline Epistles and Acts

C.J. Hemer, *The Book of Acts in the Setting of Hellenistic History* (WUNT, 49; Tübingen: J.C.B. Mohr [Paul Siebeck], 1989).

D. Slingerland, 'Acts 18.1-18, the Gallio Inscription, and Absolute Pauline Chronology', *JBL* 110 (1991), pp. 439-49.

D. Wenham, 'Acts and the Pauline Corpus II. The Evidence of Parallels', in B.W. Winter and A.D. Clarke (eds.), *The Book of Acts in its First Century Setting. I. The Book of Acts in its Ancient Literary Setting* (Carlisle: Paternoster Press, 1993), pp. 215-58.

2

THE INTEGRITY OF 2 CORINTHIANS AND ITS PLACE IN THE CORINTHIAN CORRESPONDENCE

QUESTIONS ABOUT THE INTEGRITY of the letter we now describe as 2 Corinthians are at the heart of much scholarly investigation into the work. In part this is due to questions which arise from a careful consideration of the text of the epistle itself, notably the tension that many feel exists between the tone of chs. 1–9 and that contained in chs. 10–13. As long ago as 1776 J.S. Semler, Professor of Theology at Halle, proposed that the canonical 2 Corinthians was composed of at least two originally independent letters divided along these lines, and the so-called 'Four Chapters Hypothesis', which gave formal expression to this suggestion, was first proposed by A. Hausrath in 1870. Several other incidental details might also legitimately be said to point in this direction. The fact that the name of the apostle appears only in 1.1 and 10.1 has been taken by some to indicate that originally the two sections of 2 Corinthians were independent letters. Similarly, the fact that there is a marked difference in the use of style of language between the two sections (the first person plural figures prominently in chs. 1–9 while the first person singular predominates in chs. 10–13) has also been taken as evidence supporting partition. J. Héring (1967) humorously comments about the abrupt transition from ch. 9 to ch. 10:

> When the curtain rises in 10, we are immediately aware of a complete change of scene. Titus and the Macedonians have disappeared, along with the collection-plates (p. 69).

Opinions differ as to whether chs. 10–13 were written *before*
or *after* 1–9, and are closely connected with hypothetical
reconstructions of Pauline chronology; these reconstructions
inevitably involve the juxtaposition of key texts (such as the
visit of Titus mentioned in 2 Corinthians 8 and 2 Cor. 12.17-
18) as well as a comparison of the Pauline letters with the
book of Acts. Thus, F. Watson (1984, p. 332), as part of his
spirited defence of the view that chs. 10–13 are the so-called
'tearful letter' and that they were written earlier than 1–9,
describes the alternative opinion of the relationship between
the two halves of the canonical 2 Corinthians as a theory
'based on the assumption of the incompetence of Titus'.
To summarize: chronological considerations certainly have
a key role to play in discussions about the integrity of
2 Corinthians.

Another important issue concerns the nature of ancient
letters themselves. The discovery, translation and cataloguing of thousands of ancient letters from Egypt, Greece
and the Near East has sparked off considerable interest in
this field in that it offers a database of comparative material.
As a result, there has been a veritable explosion of scholarly
study into the literary form of ancient letters, an area which
has important implications for any study of the Pauline epistles. A myriad of questions are posed: What would constitute
a letter? To what extent is it possible for a letter to substitute
for the personal presence of its author? What were the
various parts that went into constructing a letter? What was
the purpose of an address? a section of greetings? a thanksgiving? a conclusion? Was the central point of a letter always
contained within its body? Was a letter ever complete
without a parenesis? Were there standard practices used in
moving from one of these sections to another, set words or
phrases, perhaps? If so, might these be useful in identifying
how the extant letters of Paul have been put together? Does
2 Corinthians 10–13 conform to any recognizable literary
form or pattern? All of these questions, and many others,
have been the object of considerable interest among Pauline
scholars and have yielded some interesting results in recent
years. More to the point, some of the interpretative issues
concerning 2 Corinthians which have dogged scholars over

the years have had new light thrown on them by means of this important literary-critical tool. Thus, for example, L.L. Belleville (1989) has argued that 2 Cor. 1.8–7.16 is best viewed as an Hellenistic letter of recommendation, matching this form of writing in terms of both style and language. At the same time, she suggests, Paul adds a new dimension to the situation when he grounds this self-commendation in his apostolic office, no doubt as a result of the polemical situation he faces in Corinth. In short, not only are the form and structure of Paul's letters potentially made more clear, but so too is the situation which might have occasioned them.

Moreover, the debate about the unity of 2 Corinthians as it now stands has also become intertwined with scholarly discussions of 1 Corinthians and what insights that letter might offer into the nature of the correspondence between Paul and the church in Corinth. There are certain sections of the undisputed Pauline letters which indicate that 1 Corinthians may also have a more complicated textual history than is often recognized. For example, the salutations contained in Rom. 16.1-23 may well be a misplaced page of greetings which somehow became attached to the ending of the letter to the church at Rome, perhaps written from Corinth in 56–57 CE during Paul's second, or even third, visit there. There has long been a school of thought which associates the greetings of Romans 16 with the church at Ephesus based largely on complex textual considerations of Romans 14–16 and the fact that it seems somewhat odd that Paul extends greetings to so many people in the church at Rome when he has never been there before. Given these oddities it is little wonder that the church at Ephesus seems a more likely destination for these concluding verses of Romans 16. However, it is at least possible, given the fact that some of the names mentioned in the passage (Aquila and Priscilla, Gaius) are closely associated with the church at Corinth, that, properly speaking, these verses belong within the Corinthian correspondence, perhaps as a conclusion to the (lost) letter alluded to in 1 Cor. 5.9 (see below).

Establishing a chronology between 1 Corinthians and 2 Corinthians is exceedingly difficult. Much depends on how we interpret the reference in 1 Cor. 2.1 to a 'painful visit' by

Paul to the Corinthians, a visit which, incidentally, is not mentioned at all in Acts. This visit is sometimes described as Paul's 'intermediate visit' to Corinth and is commonly taken to have occurred following the composition of 1 Corinthians (although it is judged by some not to have taken place at all!). Also crucial is whether we think that chs. 10–13 were written prior to chs. 1–9, given the fact that in the former Paul twice mentions his *third* visit to the church (12.14 and 13.1) as well as his *second* visit (13.2) to Corinth. Also relevant is the interesting suggestion by G.S. Duncan (1929) that there was an eighteen-month gap between the writing of 1 Corinthians and 2 Corinthians, an argument which is based upon a specialized interpretation of Acts 20.1 and the assumption that Paul's sorrowful visit to Corinth took place sometime in this intervening period. The result is that the Corinthian correspondence has become the focus of many complex and elaborate theories of partition, each of which attempts to reconstruct the order and form of the various letters Paul wrote to the church. Needless to say, such an approach inevitably challenges the integrity of 2 Corinthians and invites its division into fragments of letters which have survived and interpolations which have been added by later Christians. Nowhere is such a fragmentation approach better illustrated than in the reconstruction offered by W. Schmithals (1973) who postulates no less than six authentically Pauline letters in 2 Corinthians (6.14–7.1; 2.14–6.2; 6.3-13 and 7.2-4; chs. 10–13; ch. 9; 1.1–2.13 and 7.5–8.24) as part of his reconstruction of the nine letters he feels were dispatched by Paul to the Corinthian church overall. At the opposite end of the spectrum are a number of commentators who accept the unity of 2 Corinthians as it now stands and who resist any such hypothetical reconstructions, offering other explanations in place of radical fragmentation theories. For example, it is sometimes suggested that Paul himself may have taken over from his amanuensis in 10.1 (as he does in Gal. 6.11), and that this is responsible for the abrupt change in tone between 1–9 and 10–13. Unfortunately, creativity usually outruns evidence in such proposals, a fact which itself stands as a testimony to the exegetical difficulties associated with 2 Corinthians as a whole.

Several factors figure within any discussion of the integrity of 2 Corinthians and we shall attempt to address them under five interrelated headings.

Earlier Correspondence between Paul and the Corinthian Church

It seems quite clear that the exchange of letters between the apostle and the Corinthians is larger than the two canonical works known to us now. In 1 Cor. 5.9 we have reference to an earlier epistle which Paul wrote to the church in which advice apparently was offered concerning ethical matters which were troubling the congregation ('I wrote to you in my letter not to associate with immoral people'). Some have attempted to identify this 'earlier epistle' with sections of the Pauline letters, notably 2 Cor. 6.14–7.1 (see below), but there remains serious doubt about the legitimacy of such an identification. However, there has been a considerable number of scholars who associate the 'earlier epistle' with another section of the canonical 2 Corinthians, an interpretation which has much more to commend it.

The 'Tearful Letter' of Paul to the Corinthians

The allusion in 1 Cor. 9.5 to an earlier letter has also been linked with the tantalizing references in 2 Cor. 2.3-4, 9 and 7.8, 12 to Paul's 'tearful letter' in an attempt to reconstruct the various stages of the Corinthian correspondence. As a result a number of scholars suggest that 2 Corinthians 10–13 is itself this 'tearful letter' which has become appended to a subsequent letter (namely 2 Cor. 1–9) sent by the apostle to the church at Corinth. One of the central planks in this reconstruction is the fact that several passages from 10–13 (notably 10.6; 13.2, 10) appear to *look forward* to the apostle's visit, whereas several passages from 1–9 (notably 2.9; 1.23; 2.3) appear to *look back* upon it; the simplest way to resolve this tension is to presume that 10–13 preceded 1–9 in terms of composition.

However, many have challenged this line of argumentation as a viable option, suggesting instead that an 'indignant

letter' might be a better description! Thus, J.L. Sumney
(1990, p. 217) notes that the interpreters who identify
2 Corinthians 10–13 as the 'earlier letter' of 2.4 usually
describe it as the 'severe letter' rather than the 'letter of
tears' which Paul mentions (he uses this as a secondary
argument against those who see an identification of 10–13 as
the 'earlier letter'). In fact, the 'tearful letter' seems to have
been written in place of an actual visit by Paul to the church;
in 2 Cor. 1.23 and 2.1 Paul says that he did not visit Corinth
in order to spare them more pain. In contrast, 10–13 seems
to have been written so as to prepare the church for an immi-
nent visit by him. This incongruity makes an outright
identification of 10–13 with the 'tearful letter' problematic in
the opinion of many interpreters. Moreover, the fact that
some passages in 2 Corinthians 10–13 seem to presuppose
sections contained in 1–9 also undermines any attempt to
view 10–13 as the 'tearful letter'. For example, A.M.G.
Stephenson (1964) insists that 12.18 refers back to events
described in chs. 8–9, notably 8.6 and 8.16-19. The meaning
of the tense of the Greek verbs contained in 2 Cor. 8.17-24
and 12.17-18 figures large in discussions of both passages
(should they be viewed as historic aorists or epistolary
aorists?). However, this is a matter about which it is impossible to come to any firm decision given our lack of knowledge
about the precise movements of Paul and his companions on
their way to and from Corinth. One recent solution is that
given by K.L. McKay (1995) who offers the interesting
suggestion that the verbs ἐξῆλθεν in 8.17 and συνεπέμψαμεν
in 8.18 are historic aorists, while συνεπέμψαμεν in 8.22 is an
epistolary aorist. The implication of this ingenious proposal
is that 2 Cor. 12.18 can be easily harmonized with 8.17-18;
both passages indicate that Titus had already been sent to
Corinth at the time that Paul was writing 2 Corinthians 1–8.
At the same time, this means that 2 Corinthians 9 could be
viewed as a separate letter which is delivered to Corinth by
means of the worthy brother (mentioned in 8.22) who is
dispatched shortly after Titus and his companion have
departed (for more on the independence of ch. 9 see below).
To clarify: if this suggestion about the sense of the aorist
verbs is correct, the three relevant phrases could be trans-

lated like this: '(Titus) *came* to you' (8.17); 'we *sent* the brother along with him (Titus)' (8.18); 'we *are sending* (the additional brother) to them (Titus and his companion)' (8.22). The implication is that the sending of the second unnamed brother in 8.22 has not yet taken place (from the standpoint of the time Paul is writing the letter), but that Paul intends to send him to Corinth shortly as the bearer of 1 Corinthians 9.

One additional question also needs to be addressed before any theory suggesting that chs. 10–13 are part of the 'tearful letter' can be said to have been proven. If chs. 10–13 are in fact an earlier stage in the Corinthian correspondence, why is it that they have come to occupy the place that they do at the end of the canonical 2 Corinthians? The most plausible explanation is that offered by G. Bornkamm (1961–62) who suggests that warning passages often appear at the end of Paul's letters (cf. 1 Cor. 16.22; Gal. 6.11-15; Rom. 16.17-20), especially in an atmosphere charged with eschatological expectations, and that a later editor of 2 Corinthians followed this pattern as he wove the various fragments together. Yet even this is something of a shot in the dark; we just do not know why the canonical 2 Corinthians ends with chs. 10–13.

For these reasons, and a number of others, it is perhaps less troublesome to posit that the (so-called) 'tearful letter' simply has not survived, than to suggest that 10–13 is this letter (or even the most important section of it). In short, the majority of scholars agree that the so-called 'earlier epistle' is lost to us, although a not insignificant number maintain that chs. 10–13 contain the substance of that letter. Having said that, it is relatively rare to find commentators writing in English who rearrange the order of the chapters of the canonical epistle in their commentaries and articles to reflect this opinion.

The Break between 2.13 and 2.14

The fact that 2.14 begins a new section of the extant 2 Corinthians and that it can arguably be said to have no obvious connection with 2.13 (where Paul mentions his jour-

ney from Troas to Macedonia in search of Titus) has given
rise to the suggestion that 2.14 is the start of another letter,
one which has survived only in fragmentary form. Generally
those who pursue this line of thought take this letter to run
from 2.14–7.4 (minus the interpolation of 6.14–7.1) and occasionally it is suggested that this section may have been part
of the so-called 'painful letter', making it the earliest
surviving fragment within 2 Corinthians. It is worth noting
that the reference to Macedonia in 7.5 serves as a nice
connection to 2.13, and has the effect of marking the boundaries of the intervening fragment of 2.14–7.4, which is sometimes described as 'the great digression'. Given this abrupt
transition from 2.13 to 2.14 there is little wonder that
J. Héring (1967, p. 16) describes the separation of 2.13 and
7.5 as 'a wide ditch'! Moreover, if the break between 2.13 and
2.14 is acknowledged and the two references to Macedonia in
2.13 and 7.5 are accepted as indicative of the intervening
interpolation, then it means that an ending for (the supposed
letter of) 1.1–2.13 is needed since it seems somehow incom-
plete otherwise. Sometimes 7.5-16 is taken to be the ending
and together the two sections (1.1–2.13 and 7.5-16) are
described as 'the letter of reconciliation'. Another possibility
is that 2.13 and 2.14 belong together (with the interpolation
running from 2.15 to 7.4?). Perhaps the strongest point in
favour of this view (beyond the fact that it does resolve the
break in continuity between 2.13 and 2.14) is that it allows a
connection of thought between 2.11 ('Satan has no advantage
over us') and 2.14 ('Thanks be to God!').

At the heart of much of this debate is the difficulty in
explaining how the thanksgiving paragraph of 2.14-17
follows on from a paragraph in which Paul explains why he
has not pursued the Christian mission in Troas and in which
he makes explicit reference to his visit to Macedonia (2.13).
Not surprisingly, there have been some attempts to identify
2.14–7.4 as the 'tearful letter' mentioned above, especially
since Paul defends his apostolic office so staunchly within
these chapters. However, there have been some recent objec-
tions to such a detachment of 2.14–7.4 from its surroundings.

For example, M.E. Thrall (1982) has argued for the unity
of 1.1–7.16 by suggesting that 2.14 marks the beginning of a

fresh thanksgiving section of the epistle rather than the introduction of an originally independent letter. Thrall is here modifying the oft-repeated suggestion that it was the good news Paul received from Titus about the Corinthians' reception of his earlier letter which occasions the outburst of thanksgiving. The suggestion frequently put forward is that mention of Titus in 2.13 causes Paul to recollect his encounter with his fellow-worker, and the good news which Titus was able to bring, which in turn gives rise to the exultant outburst which is responsible for the awkward break between 2.13 and 2.14. This is certainly a possible explanation, although it is hampered somewhat by the fact that Paul nowhere here says explicity that he ever managed to catch up with Titus and receive this good news. However, as Thrall goes on to note, the vocabulary and subject-matter of 2.14-17 is different from that of 7.6-13 (the former, she says, is the language of evangelization and the latter is the language of consolation). All of this, Thrall contends, undermines the suggestion that Titus's news was responsible for the fresh thanksgiving section of 2.14-17. On the contrary, that 2.14-17 could be considered as a thanksgiving section, and that it is original to the letter which commenced at 1.1, seems indicated when the paragraph is examined against structural analyses of how thanksgiving sections functioned in the Pauline letters as a whole. Far from concentrating on the awkward break in thought which seems to exist between 2.13 and 2.14, Thrall argues that we are perhaps nearer the mark if we take the thanksgiving section of 2.14-17 as an introduction to the material which follows in 3.1-7.16. This approach has important implications for the unity of ch. 7 as well, for one of the supporting reasons for Thrall's interpretation of the whole of 1.1-7.16 as a unity is the fact that she sees no necessity for a break between 7.4 and 7.5. Thus the suggestion (made by Schmithals and a host of others) that 7.5-16 be detached from 7.4 is considered untenable. Nevertheless, there are features of Thrall's interpretation which leave much to be desired, not least its inability to explain the tension between Paul's evangelistic failure in Troas and God's ultimate triumph 'always and everywhere' noted in 2.14.

Similarly, S.J. Hafemann (1990) argues for the unity of
chs. 1–7 and suggests that the abrupt transition from 2.13 to
2.14 can be explained by recognizing the central place that
the triumph imagery contained in 2.14-16a has within these
chapters. Once the cause of Paul's joyful outburst in 2.14-16a
is understood, namely, that he rejoices in the paradoxical
weakness of being an apostle, then the trials and tribulations
mentioned in 1.3-11, the anguish over his painful visit
mentioned in 2.4, and his worry over Titus mentioned in
2.12-13, are all of one piece. In short, the 'break' between
2.13 and 2.14 is really non-existent; instead 2.14-16 is the
logical response to the example of apostolic suffering given in
2.12-13. Thus, Hafemann concludes that due attention to
Paul's understanding of the nature of his apostolic ministry
resolves the tension between 2.13 and 2.14.

The Independence of Chapter 9

Some modern interpreters follow the suggestion first put
forward by Semler in 1776 and argue that ch. 9 was originally an independent letter in its own right. There are
several reasons for such a suggestion, including the place
that the chapter has within the reconstructed chronology of
Paul's life and the fact that the chapter appears to prepare
the way for Paul's visit to Achaia (see 9.2). Most importantly,
many have remarked upon how incongruous it is for Paul to
have written in 9.1, 'Now it is superfluous for me to write to
you about the offering for the saints' (RSV), when he has just
spent the whole of the previous chapter doing precisely that,
namely, commending the churches to contribute to the collection for the poor in Jerusalem. Indeed, one of the most
dubious features of 9.1 is the unusual Greek phrase with
which it begins ($\pi\epsilon\rho\grave{\iota}$ $\mu\grave{\epsilon}\nu$ $\gamma\grave{\alpha}\rho$). Largely on the basis of this
phrase H. Windisch (1924) and H.D. Betz (1985) argue for the
independence of both 2 Corinthians 9 *and* 2 Corinthians 8,
interpreting both chapters as administrative letters written
by Paul in connection with the collection and serving to
communicate his travel plans to Corinth and environs. Most
commonly, however, it is the independence of ch. 9 which has
been the focus of scholarly attention with ch. 8 generally

regarded as integral to the letter contained in 2 Corinthians
1–8.

In light of these considerations it is hardly surprising that
a number of suggestions have been put forward which take
ch. 9 to have been a separate letter, with a correspondingly
diverse range of opinions having been offered as to when ch.
9 was penned in relation to chs. 1–8. Some have suggested
ch. 9 *precedes* the writing of chs. 1–8 in that Paul uses the
generosity of the churches in Achaia as a basis for boasting
to the Macedonians (9.2) in an attempt to get them to contribute as liberally to the collection (8.1-5). Thus, J. Héring
(1967) argues that the writing of ch. 9 precedes that of ch. 8
by suggesting that in 9.3-4 it appears that Paul originally
intends to accompany Titus and the brethren from
Macedonia in their journey to pick up the collection. In ch. 8
this does not happen, which seems to suggest that between
the writing of the two letters Paul has changed his mind.
However, this argument can easily be turned on its head and
ch. 9 taken to *follow* chs. 1–8 with the liberality of the
Macedonians (8.1-5) serving as an example for the churches
in Achaia (9.2). So R. Jewett (1978) suggests that originally
2 Corinthians 9 followed the writing of 2 Corinthians 10–13
but that it was placed in its present position by a later
redactor (perhaps at the time of the writing of the Pastoral
epistles?). Whatever else may be said about the relationship
between ch. 9 and the preceding chapters, the rough transition from 8.24 to 9.1 does present some problems which
invite explanation. The humorous suggestion by F.F. Bruce
(1971) that there was a short break in dictation at this point,
during which fresh news of the situation arrives via Titus, is
but one possible solution. Having said that, many recent
commentators do not feel that the tension between chs. 1-8
and 9 is sufficient to warrant the postulation of the independence of ch. 9 and argue instead for the unity of 1–9. Perhaps
we do not go far wrong if we suggest that ch. 9 was written at
about the same time as chs. 1–8, but with a different audience in mind (chs. 1–8 appear to have been directed to the
church in Corinth and ch. 9 to the churches of Achaia). We
could follow D. Georgi (1992) and go so far as to suggest that
ch. 8 was written from Philippi and ch. 9 from Thessalonica,

although this is by no means a certainty. Occasionally it has been suggested that the benediction of 13.11-14 was the original ending of the letter embodied in chs. 1–9 and that 10.1–13.12 were inserted in the course of the transmission of the text.

The Interpolation of 6.14–7.1

Several features of the curious paragraph contained in 2 Cor. 6.14–7.1 have made it the focus of much scholarly investigation. Structurally the paragraph is self-contained and can stand as an independent unit, although there is no manuscript evidence which suggests that it had an independent existence or that 2 Corinthians ever stood without it. The passage has frequently been identified with the 'earlier epistle' which Paul alludes to in 1 Cor. 5.9, largely because it adopts a rather strict attitude concerning relationships with unbelievers. The paragraph commences with an exhortation not to be yoked with unbelievers and follows this up with a call for the faithful to be separated from impurity. Five rhetorical questions are then posed and these are substantiated by a testimonia of Old Testament quotes (from Lev. 26.12; Ezek. 20.34; 37.27; Isa. 52.11; 2 Sam. 7.14) which are adduced as scriptural proofs of the principle of separation. Not only does the paragraph appear to break the flow of the argument of the letter (which carries on nicely from 6.13 to 7.2), but the parenesis of the paragraph in 6.14–7.1 seems wholly unrelated to the surrounding context of the Corinthian epistle.

The awkwardness of establishing a context for the passage, coupled with the fact that an unusually high number of Pauline *hapax legomena* appear in these six verses (some nine in all including Βελιάρ in 6.15), and the fact that some apparently non-Pauline understandings of key Pauline ideas also appear (the contrast between δικαιοσύνη and ἀνομία in 6.14 being a case in point), has led many to regard the paragraph as a non-Pauline fragment which has been inserted into a genuine Pauline letter. In the oft-quoted words of N.A. Dahl:

If the fragment had recently been discovered on a sheet of papyrus, the idea of Pauline authorship would hardly have occurred to anybody (1977, p. 63).

The dualism inherent in the passage, alongside the 'community as temple' motif in 6.16 and the strict call for the separation of the righteous from those who are contaminated by the world, has prompted some interesting comparisons with key Qumran materials, notably 1QS, 1QM, 1QH and 4QFlor. The curious reference in 6.15 to the Hebrew word *beliar* as a name for the Satanic adversary of God also points in this direction. In addition to its frequent appearance in such Jewish texts as *The Testament of the Twelve Patriarchs* (*T. Jos.* 7.4; *T. Jud.* 25.3; *T. Iss.* 6.1; 7.7; *T. Levi* 18.12-13; 19.1; *T. Zeb.* 9.8) and *Jubilees* (1.20; 15.33), the title appears in a number of texts from Qumran including 1QS 1.18, 24; 2.19; 1QM 13.1-4 and 1QH 6.21. Few would go so far as to suggest that the fragment of 6.14–7.1 was itself written by an Essene, but many agree that it clearly shows an affinity to some of the ideas found within the Qumran community. If so, the author was probably not an Essene, but an unknown Christian who was familiar with the mindset of the Essenes and reworked some of their ideas into this fragment which (mysteriously) has come to be included within the canonical 2 Corinthians. Thus R.P. Martin (1986), for example, accepts an Essene source behind the fragment but argues that Paul himself inserted it into his letter.

Despite these many difficulties associated with 6.14–7.1, a growing number of commentators concludes that there is a continuity in Paul's argument and that there is no compelling reason for denying that the paragraph is authentically Pauline. This number includes J.-F. Collange (1972) in his highly creative proposal that Paul composed *two* versions of the epistle which commenced at 2.14, one of which he suggests concluded with 6.14–7.1). Understandably, there have been several attempts to explain why it is that Paul, or the unknown author (or editor), saw fit to add the fragment where he did. Six of the more recent suggestions are worth noting briefly, if for no other reason than that they demonstrate the lengths to which scholars are driven to try and force a connection between the surrounding sections of the

epistle and the interpolation itself, in much the same way
that one might attempt to force a piece of a jigsaw puzzle into
a given spot despite the fact that it does not quite seem to fit.
Several of these explanations appeal to external sources and
materials in an attempt to solve the mystery of 6.14–7.1.
   The first example is that of G.D. Fee (1977) who questions
whether 6.14–7.1 really does represent a radical departure
from mainstream Pauline thought. He does this mainly by
comparing 6.14–7.1 with 1 Cor. 3.16-17 and 1 Cor. 8–10,
where the ethical dilemma about whether Christian
believers should join unbelievers in eating meat offered to
idols is discussed. Fee concludes that in both passages from
1 Corinthians there is a call for separation, which, in the
final analysis, is not dissimilar to that found in 6.14–7.1.
The key thing to note here is how an external source
(1 Corinthians) is used to explain the place and purpose of
6.14–7.1; the awkward passage is best interpreted by setting
it within the larger framework of Paul's dealings with the
church at Corinth.
   The second example is that of J. Lambrecht (1978) who
freely acknowledges how closely related 2 Cor. 6.11-13 and
7.2-4 are in terms of tone, content and style and the fact that
6.14–7.1 is markedly different on all counts. The crucial
questions remain: to what degree does 6.14–7.1 disrupt the
flow of the passage, and why is it inserted? Lambrecht does
not feel that too much should be made of the disruption idea
since Paul frequently interrupts himself in the course of his
arguments. Beyond that, both 6.13 and 6.14 contain impera-
tive verbs in the second person plural (πλατύνθητε and γίνεσθε
respectively) and it is relatively easy to see how one exhortation might flow into the other. The manner of Old Testament
citation in the passage is not of much help in deciding the
matter either in that it conforms to Paul's general practice
elsewhere. The net result is that, after an exhaustive exami-
nation of both the form and content of 6.14–7.1, Lambrecht
can find nothing which requires the passage to be adjudged
non-Pauline.
   The third example is that of J. Murphy-O'Connor (1987)
who argues that Paul had Deut. 11.13-15 in the back of his
mind when he began the paragraph ending in 2 Cor. 6.10 and

that he made an associative jump in the next verse to another Old Testament passage (Deut. 6.11) which provided the basis for the ethical exhortation commencing in 2 Cor. 6.11. If we then take 2 Cor. 6.12-13 simply to be a slight digression, we can see how the exhortation contained in Deut. 6.11 has paved the way for the similar exhortation given by Paul in 6.14–7.1. Murphy-O'Connor next calls attention to the references to δικαιοσύνη (as opposed to ἀνομία) in 6.14 and suggests that this reflects the thought contained in Deut. 11.13 which is then summarized in 2 Cor. 7.1 at the conclusion of the paragraph. In short, the associations with key Old Testament texts from Deuteronomy cause Paul's thoughts to leap from point to point in a logical (but not readily visible) fashion. When written down, and later read, the passage looks like an interpolation simply because we have not been able easily to follow the unconscious connections of thought. According to Murphy-O'Connor (1988) the way that Philo of Alexandria handles the concept of 'unbelief' may also be of relevance here, providing a parallel to Paul's concerns regarding the ideas of his opponents in Corinth. Regardless of whether or not such a suggestion is correct, it does demonstrate how extra-biblical sources are being called upon to try and solve the difficulties of 2 Cor. 6.14–7.1.

The fourth example is that of J.D.M. Derrett (1978), which is similar to that of J. Murphy-O'Connor in that it uses the Old Testament quotations and allusions contained in the passage to explain how 6.14–7.4 fits into the letter. For Derrett, however, the Old Testament passages under consideration are Lev. 19.19, a statement about the inter-marriage of Jews and foreigners, and Deut. 22.10, a statement which prohibits ploughing with an ox and ass yoked together. Both do offer a context for the exhortation of separation with which 6.14 begins ('do not be yoked'), but Derrett feels that it is Deut. 22.10, rather than the more commonly accepted prohibition of Lev. 19.19, that Paul really has in mind when he composes the awkward paragraph. The prohibition against yoking an ox with an ass, in addition to its literal sense, can carry a metaphorical meaning as well. But what is the point of Paul using such a metaphor? What sort of unequal 'yoking' does he wish to discourage? Derrett finds the answer to be a financial one, and suggests that Paul here is questioning the wisdom *of his entering into financial partnership with the Corinthians.* In support of this rather forced interpretation of an Old Testament allusion, Derrett points to several passages in 2 Corinthians, notably 8.8-15, which show Paul aggressively responding to suggestions that he has cheated the Corinthians over the gathering of money for the Jerusalem collection. It is worth mentioning that Derrett takes the ἄπιστοι of 6.15 to mean 'ones who are financially untrustworthy'. This is a novel, if somewhat bizarre, departure from the way the term is normally used in Paul's letters, but there may be a parallel in Jesus' statement recorded in Lk 16.10-12.

The fifth example is that of W.J. Webb (1993) who concentrates upon the exhortations in 6.17 ('come out from the midst of them and be separate' (ἐξέλθατε ἐκ μέσου αὐτῶν καὶ ἀφορίσθητε). Webb argues that this call to 'come out' and to 'be separate' is reminiscent of both the Old Testament exodus motif and the return from exile theme and allows us to tie the whole of 6.14–7.1 into Paul's new covenant theology, inarguably one of his most central themes in 2 Corinthians. Central to Webb's hypothesis is the suggestion that Paul identifies himself as the *ʿebed Yahweh* in calling the Corinthians to return home to the bonds of the new covenant (this is done mainly by appeal to Isa. 49.8-9 as setting up a conceptual bridge to 6.14–7.1). The result is that the (so-called) interpolation is seen to be perfectly compatible with 2 Cor. 2.14–7.4 where the idea of the new covenant in Christ lies at the heart of much of Paul's argument.

Finally, the interesting, but highly speculative, interpretation offered by H.D. Betz (1973) that 6.14–7.1 is in fact an anti-Pauline passage reflecting the theology of Paul's opponents in Galatia is also worth mentioning. Betz's case hinges upon his suggestion that the author of the paragraph is exhorting his readership 'not to become associated with unbelievers' (μὴ γίνεσθε ἑτεροζυγοῦντες ἀπίστοις), *such as Paul,* because the apostle was felt by the author of the fragment to have forsaken a lifestyle which is lived under the regulations of the Torah. However, this suggestion offers no credible explanation as to how and why a Pauline editor came to insert it into the apostolic 2 Corinthians, having failed to recognize its anti-Pauline sentiment or know of its anti-Pauline origin. Consequently, Betz's idea has not attracted much scholarly support.

Note: Many commentators attempt to reflect the complex nature of the Corinthian correspondence by identifying the various sections of the epistles with a letter and proposing a hypothetical order. A common assessment of the letters and their chronological relationship looks something like this:

Letter Contents	When Written	Relevant References

Founding Visit by Paul in 50–52
Accompanied by Timothy and Silvanus (Acts 18.1-18; 2 Cor. 1.19)

A Probably Lost (but perhaps 2 Cor. 6.14–7.1 is a fragment)	Summer of 52	1 Cor. 5.9

Painful visit by Paul from Ephesus in Summer of 53
(Not recorded in Acts but alluded to in 2 Cor. 2.1 and 12.21)

The Corinthians write a letter to Paul (1 Cor. 7.1) which is probably delivered by Stephanas, Fortunatus and Achaicus (1 Cor. 16.15-18)

B 1 Corinthians	Autumn of 53 from Ephesus Delivered by Stephanas Fortunatus and Achaicus (?)	1 Cor. 16.8 1 Cor. 16.17
C Now Lost (The 'Letter of Tears')	Summer of 54 from Ephesus Delivered by Titus (?)	2 Cor. 2.4; 7.5-8
D 2 Cor. 1–9 (minus 6.14–7.1)	Autumn of 54 from Macedonia Delivered by Titus (?)	
E 2 Cor. 10–13	Spring of 55 from Macedonia Delivered by Unknown Person(s) (but presumably not Titus because of the internal reference to him)	2 Cor. 12.17-18

2 Corinthians

*Final Visit by Paul from Macedonia in early Spring of 56
(Acts 20.2-3; Rom. 15.25-26; 2 Cor. 10.6; 13.2, 10).*

*The Delivery of the Collection to Jerusalem and Paul's Arrest in late
Spring of 56 (Acts 20.6-7, 16; 21.17-19, 30-33; Rom. 15.30-31)*

In any event, it must be remembered that 2 Corinthians
presents the interpreter with a host of historical and exegetical problems, which in turn give rise to a number of other
possibilities. For example, the question of whether
1 Corinthians was written before or after Paul's second visit
to Corinth remains a problem which continues to divide
scholarship. Similarly, the precise division of 2 Corinthians
remains something of a scholarly free-for-all. The inability of
scholars to arrive at a clear consensus about these matters is
one of the abiding fascinations, and frustrations(!), of a study
of 2 Cor. A convenient place to find a systematic presentation
of the various options is J.M. Gilchrist, 'Paul and the
Corinthians—The Sequence of Letters and Visits', *JSNT* 34
(1988), pp. 47-69.

Suggestions for Further Reading

On Epistolary Form and Purpose
D.E. Aune, *The New Testament in its Literary Environment* (Cambridge:
James Clark, 1987), pp. 158-225.
L.L. Belleville, 'A Letter of Apologetic Self-Commendation: 2 Cor. 1.8–7.16',
NovT 31 (1989), pp. 142-63.
R. Funk, 'The Apostolic Parousia: Form and Significance', in W.R. Farmer,
C.F.D. Moule and R.R. Niebuhr (eds.), *Christian History and
Interpretation: Studies Presented to John Knox* (Cambridge: Cambridge
University Press, 1967), pp. 249-68.
J. Murphy-O'Connor, *Paul the Letter-Writer: His World, his Options, his
Skills* (Collegeville, MN: Liturgical Press, 1995).

On Partition Theories and the Integrity of 2 Corinthians
W.H. Bates, 'The Integrity of II Corinthians', *NTS* 12 (1965–66), pp. 56-69.
R. Batey, 'Paul's Interaction with the Corinthians', *JBL* 84 (1965), pp. 139-
46.
G. Bornkamm, 'The History of the Origin of the So-Called Second Letter to
the Corinthians', *NTS* 8 (1961–62), pp. 258-64.
K.L. McKay, 'Observations on the Epistolary Aorist in 2 Corinthians', *NovT*
37 (1995), pp. 154-58.
R. Jewett, 'The Redaction of 1 Corinthians and the Trajectory of the Pauline
School', *JAAR* 44 (1978), pp. 389-444.

W. Schmithals, 'Die Korintherbriefe als Briefsammlung', *ZNW* 64 (1973), pp. 263-88.

A.M.G. Stephenson, 'Partition Theories on II Corinthians', *SE* 2 (1964), pp. 639-46.

—'A Defence of the Integrity of 2 Corinthians', in *The Authorship and Integrity of the New Testament* (SPCK Theological Collections, 4; London: SPCK, 1965), pp. 82-97.

N.H. Taylor, 'The Composition and Chronology of Second Corinthians', *JSNT* 44 (1991), pp. 67-87.

On Chapters 10–13 as the 'Tearful Letter' of 2 Cor. 2.3-4, 9 and 7.8, 12

L.L. Welborn, 'The Identification of 2 Corinthians 10–13 with the "Letter of Tears"', *NovT* 37 (1995), pp. 138-53.

On the Break between 2 Cor. 2.13 and 2.14

J. Murphy-O'Connor, 'Paul and Macedonia: The Connection between 2 Corinthians 2.13 and 2.14', *JSNT* 25 (1985), pp. 99-103.

M.E. Thrall, 'A Second Thanksgiving Period in II Corinthians', *JSNT* 16 (1982), pp. 101-24.

On 2 Cor. 6.14–7.1

H.D. Betz, '2 Cor. 6.14–7.1. An Anti-Pauline Fragment?', *JBL* 92 (1973), pp. 88-108.

J.D.M. Derrett, '2 Cor 6,14ff. A Midrash on Dt 22,10', *Bib* 59 (1978), pp. 231-50.

G.D. Fee, 'II Corinthians VI.14–VII.1 and Food Offered to Idols', *NTS* 23 (1977), pp. 140-61.

J.A. Fitzmyer, 'Qumran and the Interpolated Paragraph in 2 Cor. 6.14–7.1', *CBQ* 23 (1961), pp. 271-80. [Reprinted in *Essays on The Semitic Background of the New Testament* (London: Geoffrey Chapman, 1971), pp. 205-17.]

J. Gnilka, '2 Cor. 6.14–7.1 in the Light of the Qumran Texts and the Testaments of the Twelve Patriarchs', in J. Murphy-O'Connor (ed.), *Paul and Qumran: Studies in New Testament Exegesis* (London: Geoffrey Chapman, 1968), pp. 48-68.

J.C. Hurd, *The Origin of 1 Corinthians* (London: SPCK, 1965), pp. 235-37.

J.L. Lambrecht, 'The Fragment 2 Cor. vi 14-vii 1. A Plea for its Authenticity', in T. Baarda, A.F.J. Klijn and W.C. van Unnik (eds.), *Miscellanea Neotestamentica*, II (NovTSup, 47; Leiden: Brill, 1978), pp. 143-61.

J. Murphy-O'Connor, 'Relating 2 Corinthians 6.14–7.1 to its Context', *NTS* 33 (1987), pp. 272-75.

—'Philo and 2 Cor. 6.14–7.1', *RB* 95 (1988), pp. 55-69.

M.E. Thrall, 'The Problem of II Cor. VI.14–VII.1 in Some Recent Discussion', *NTS* 24 (1978), pp. 132-48.

W.J. Webb, *Returning Home: New Covenant and Second Exodus as the Context for 2 Corinthians 6.14–7.1* (JSNTSup, 85; Sheffield: JSOT Press, 1993).

3

THE APOSTOLIC
MINISTRY OF PAUL

THE TERM 'APOSTLE' (ἀπόστολος) is used six times within
2 Corinthians (1.1; 8.23; 11.5, 13; 12.11, 12), a fact which in
itself stands as some measure of the importance that the
apostolic ministry has for Paul's thought within the letter.
Elsewhere, in the undisputed letters of Paul, 'apostle' is used
a total of seventeen times, usually as a self-reference; in
three of these instances (Rom. 1.1; 1 Cor. 1.1; Gal. 1.1) it
appears as part of the introductory greeting. The precise
meaning and background of the term has been the subject of
considerable discussion, particularly as it relates to the question of the identification of Paul's Corinthian opponents.
W. Schmithals (1969) and C.K. Barrett (1978) offer some of
the most extensive treatments of the matter, with the former
stressing Gnosticism (and Antioch!) as the base for the
concept of apostleship and the latter stressing the Jewish
idea of an envoy, a *shaliah* (and Jerusalem!) as its origin.

While the role of an apostle is one of the central ideas
governing Paul's understanding of Christian mission, it
seems clear that the idea of an established apostleship did
not originate with him. It also seems evident that from the
beginning of the Christian movement the apostles were a
group larger than the twelve disciples, and that being a
witness to the resurrection of Jesus Christ was considered
significant in the definition of an apostle (see 1 Cor. 9.1; 15.3-
8; Acts 1.22). At the same time there are some indications
that the term 'apostle' was also occasionally used by Paul in

a non-technical sense. For example, he uses it in 2 Cor. 8.23
to refer to the two brothers sent with Titus to Corinth with
specific responsibility to facilitate the collection for the saints
in Jersualem (the translation of ἀπόστολοι as 'messengers' in
the RSV is an indication of the non-technical meaning that
the term could carry; also note the use of ἀπόστολος with
reference to Epaphroditus in Phil. 2.25).

The question of Paul's authority as an apostle is without
doubt central to any interpretation of 2 Corinthians.
However, having doubts raised about his apostleship was by
no means a new issue for Paul, especially if, as N.A. Dahl
(1977) suggests, the earlier 1 Cor. 1.10–4.21 is to be taken as
an apology for Paul's apostolic ministry. In addition, it may
well be that in 2 Cor. 1.17-24 we catch a glimpse of Paul's
integrity as an apostle being called into question because he
did not keep his word about visiting Corinth as he had
proposed in 1 Cor. 16.5-7. Thus, he may have appeared to
some Corinthians as untrustworthy, saying both 'Yes! I am
coming!' and 'No! I am not coming!' at the same time. Alternatively, the passage could indicate that the Corinthians
thought that Paul was inconsistent in his proclamation of the
essence of the gospel among them, first stressing the risen
and glorified Lord who embodies the wisdom of God (as in
2 Cor. 4.6), and then emphasizing the shame of the cross (as
in 1 Cor. 1.23 and 2.2). Or, again, it could reflect Corinthian
opinion over Paul's seemingly contradictory attitudes
to financial support, that is to say, Paul's willingness to
accept the help of the Macedonian churches while at the
same time stubbornly, even arrogantly, refusing to allow the
Corinthians to assist him. Each of these possibilities has its
advocates and it is very difficult, even unwise, to decide
between them, since one reason for the Corinthians' dissatis-
faction could readily become entangled with others. On
balance, though, the context of the passage favours Paul's
failure to keep his promise about visiting the Corinthians as
the precipitating reason for their complaints. It is likely that
a formal complaint of some sort was lodged about Paul's conduct, as he uses the technical term ἐλαφρία (translated in the
RSV by the verb 'vacillating') in 1.17 (it only appears here in
the whole of the New Testament), perhaps echoing the actual

charge made by the Corinthians against him (based on Jesus'
statement in Mt. 5.17?). The presence of the article accompa-
nying the term would seem so to suggest (Moffatt indicates
this by translating the word as 'fickle' and placing it in
quotes).

Despite our inability to determine precisely why Paul finds
it necessary to counter the charge of vacillation in 2 Cor.
1.17-24, there are a number of other passages which clearly
indicate that he was concerned over Corinthian doubts about
his apostolic standing. For example, 2 Cor. 10.12-18 is seen
by many to be central to any discussion of Paul's apostolic
ministry, and most discussions of the subject concentrate on
this pericope, largely under the influence of E. Käsemann's
interpretation of the passage. It is often linked to Gal. 2.1-10
where an agreed division of apostolic labour and territory
seems indicated; Paul understood his calling to be the
'apostle to the Gentiles' (εἰμι ἐγώ ἐθνῶν ἀπόστολος, Rom. 11.13)
and defined his apostolic role largely in terms of his ministry
among non-Jews outside of Palestine. It seems clear that
Paul understood his authority as an apostle to be inextri-
cably related to his calling to preach the gospel of Christ
(Rom. 1.1; Gal. 1.15-17). As J.H. Schütz (1975, p. 36) puts the
point: 'The terms "apostle" and "gospel" are more than just
intimately connected; they are functionally related'. Thus
when we come to discuss Paul's understanding of the gospel
of Jesus Christ we inevitably find ourselves discussing his
perception of apostleship at the same time.

Paul's Opponents

Several things may be deduced about the nature of the
Corinthian opponents' understanding of apostolic ministry
based on Paul's response to them in 2 Corinthians. However,
it must be emphasized that the reconstruction of what the
Corinthian opponents believed and taught is difficult to
reconstruct with any degree of precision since it only comes
to us channelled through Paul himself. The situation is a bit
like listening to one side of a telephone conversation and
trying to deduce the remarks made on the other end of the
line based upon what you hear at your end; it goes without

saying that such a situation is hardly a guarantee for accuracy of perception! However, there is general agreement that the Corinthian opponents asserted their own rights and position and challenged Paul's apostleship on several different accounts. Let us list some of these areas, each of which elicited a sharp response from Paul:

They Had Specific Letters of Commendation
The opponents of Paul apparently came brandishing letters of recommendation to the church at Corinth (2 Cor. 3.1; cf. 4.2; 5.12; 6.4; 10.12, 18; 12.11). By whom had such letters been granted and for what purpose? Were they issued by James and the church at Jerusalem, perhaps as one of the conditions of the Jerusalem Council? Or could it be that a commendatory letter was issued by the church at Ephesus in support of the ministry of Apollos in Corinth (as F. Watson 1986, pp. 80-87 suggests)? More to the point, were the intruders who had these letters in their possession Judaizers wishing to impose their particular understanding of the Christian faith upon the Corinthian believers? If so, then it is easy to see why these letters of recommendation (specifically mentioned in 3.1) become one of the major points of disagreement between Paul and his rivals in Corinth. It is also easy to envisage how readily the matter might become embroiled in the larger issue of the nature of Paul's apostolic ministry. Indeed, W. Baird (1961) takes the whole of 3.1-3 to be concerned with Paul's discussion of apostolic authority (rather than with the letters of recommendation as such) and offers an attractive interpretation of 3.2 in which the textual variant 'our' (ἡμῶν) is adopted instead of the generally accepted 'your' (ὑμῶν). This has the effect of switching the direction of the image so that the Corinthian church is the epistle written on Paul's heart by Christ himself—an interpretation which lends itself more readily, so Baird argues, to the larger discussion of apostolic authority. Many interpreters accept Baird's suggestion, despite the reading adopted by the RSV.

The ingenuity of Paul's argument in 2 Cor. 3.1-3 is impressive and amply demonstrates his ability to bend an argument to suit his own purposes. He cleverly links the question of the legitimacy of his apostleship with the legitimacy of the Corinthian church as a Christian community. They cannot deny his apostleship without calling into question their own existence as part of the body of Christ; to reject the messenger (Paul) is to despise the message (the gospel). Paul asserts that the Corinthians themselves are his letter, and as such stand in contrast to the written letters brandished by the opponents who have infiltrated the church.

In summary, the precise meaning of 'letters of recommendation' (συστατικῶν ἐπιστολῶν) is much debated, but it appears to mean not only letters of recommendation to the Corinthian church (from Jerusalem?) but letters of recommendation from them to others (especially if 'from you' [ἐξ ὑμῶν] at the end of 3.1 is given its full weight).

They Belittled Paul's Physical Appearance and Called into Question his Oratorical Skill
There is every indication that the Corinthian congregation was predisposed toward a high-profile, sensationalistic ministry which laid stress on charismatic leadership and emphasized the importance of spiritual gifts in the lives of the members. Much of 1 Corinthians is given over to discussing the proper place of such matters within the life of the church, notably 1 Corinthians 12–14. Ironically, it appears that Paul himself fell foul of such an assessment of what was truly important for an apostolic ministry and that this was of no little significance in their controversy with him. In the eyes of his opponents Paul did not have what it took to be an apostle, or at least not a very charismatic one. Indeed, Paul's passing remark about the 'signs of an apostle' (τὰ μὲν σημεῖα τοῦ ἀποστόλου) in 2 Cor. 12.12 may be his quoting one of the slogans used by the opponents against him back at them. In 2 Cor. 10.10 we have an even clearer indication of the opponents' opinion of him. Paul writes: 'For they say, "His letters are weighty and strong, but his bodily presence is weak, and his speech of no account" '. Paul accepts such criticisms of his human abilities, but makes them work to his advantage in the course of the argument, effectively turning the tables on his opponents and using their criticisms of him against them. Boasting of his human weakness and failure becomes the

focus of Paul's reply to the Corinthians insofar as it provides opportunity for God's grace in Christ to be made manifest. It is quite striking that forms of the verb 'I boast' (καυχάομαι) appear some 19 times in 2 Corinthians 10–13. Paul's boast that human weakness is paradoxically God's strength is given a christological foundation in 10.1, the opening statement of his most strident defence of apostleship (chs. 10–13). Here Paul entreats the Corinthians to recall 'the meekness and gentleness of Christ' (πραΰτητος καὶ ἐπιεικείας τοῦ Χριστοῦ), a phrase designed to assert that the lowliness and weakness of the Lord is the basis for his own ministry as an apostle.

This note of human weakness comes through again in 2 Cor. 13.3-4, but here it is linked to the crucifixion of Christ and declared to be overturned by the paradox of the cross and the power of the resurrection. Here Paul declares that such resurrection power is able to absorb human weakness, even his! It is on this basis that he feels confident of his apostolic authority in dealing with the Corinthians. Similarly, in 2 Cor. 11.6 Paul acknowledges that he might be described as 'unskilled in speaking' (ἰδιώτης τῷ λόγῳ), a confession perhaps made in deliberate contrast to Apollos who was thought to be gifted in such matters and probably fluent in Greek (cf. 1 Cor. 1.12; 3.4-6; cf. Acts 18.24-25). Throughout there is a deliberate contrast between God's power and human weakness being asserted by Paul. Indeed, it is significant that his reply to the assertion of authority based on power or ability or prestige is an emphasis on suffering for the cross of Christ. Thus, no less than four times in 2 Corinthians he catalogues some of the hardships and affliction he has endured as an apostle (4.8-9; 6.4-5; 11.23-29; 12.10; cf. 1 Cor. 4.9-13 and Rom. 8.35), freely inserting reference to them in the course of his argument. Thus affliction (θλῖψις) becomes a dominant theme in the letter (1.4, 6, 8; 2.4; 4.8; 8.13). For Paul, ministry was exercised in the midst of weakness, and suffering in the name of Christ was an important witness to his apostleship. D.A. Black (1984) stresses the significance of the idea of 'weakness' for Paul's apostolic defence when he concludes his study of the theme with these words:

For Paul weakness is the greatest sign of apostleship because it identifies him in a plain way with his crucified Master. Through weakness the power of the resurrection finds its fullest expression in the apostle, in his apostolic mission, and in the communities he founded. Christ's power is present with Paul in his weakness and with all those whom the Spirit of Christ indwells (p. 253).

They Stressed their Right to Financial Support from the Churches they Served

Apparently the 'superstar apostles' of Corinth (to use F.W. Danker's description of them) took it as their right that they should receive financial support from the congregation(s) they served. From 1 Cor. 9.1-18 it appears that Paul's refusal to accept such payment was taken by some in Corinth to undermine his claim to be an apostle (a similar controversy is addressed in 1 Thess. 2.3-12 and 2 Thess. 3.6-13). In short, apostleship and fiscal responsibility are intricately tied together in Paul's mind and he apparently regarded financial independence as part of his legitimacy as an apostle. This may well have defied social conventions of patronage, offending some of the wealthy members of the congregation and contributing to the tensions between Paul and the church at Corinth. On the other hand, it may be Paul asserting the conventions of benevolence, whereby a leading figure in a given community was expected not to be a burden to that community. In any event, it seems that the questions of financial independence and apostolic authority were intertwined in Paul's dispute with his opponents at Corinth and, if 1 Cor. 4.12 and 9.1-18 are anything to go by, had been so from the beginning of Paul's founding mission in Corinth. We may detect a further echo of Paul's dispute with the Corinthians over his financial independence in 2 Cor. 2.17. 'we are not, like so many, peddlers of God's word'. Paul is here contrasting his own style of proclaiming the gospel with that of his opponents and insists that he does so out of sincerity (implying that they do so out of insincerity).

They Asserted their Place within the Establishment of Christian Faith in Corinth and Challenged the Gospel which Paul Proclaimed

It seems clear that Paul's place as the founder of the church at Corinth was challenged by his Corinthian opponents. In response, Paul stresses his fatherly concern for the congregation in such passages as 2 Cor. 6.13, 10.14-15, 11.2-4 and 12.14 (cf. the all-important precursor to this idea contained in 1 Cor. 4.14-21). Much more worrying (from Paul's perspective) is the fact that the opponents were undermining the gospel message which the apostle had proclaimed among the Corinthians when he founded the church there. We see this particularly set out in 2 Cor. 11.4, one of Paul's most biting and satirical comments: 'For if someone comes and preaches another Jesus than the one we preached, or if you receive a different spirit from the one you received, or if you accept a different gospel from the one you accepted, you submit to it readily enough'. Precisely what this other gospel message was, and what new slant on the person of Jesus, or the nature of Christian living, it proclaimed, are matters of much recent debate. Undoubtedly Paul is concerned about the present willingness on the part of the Corinthians to be open to new ideas, and the challenge this presents to the true proclamation of the gospel which he imparted to them when founding the church there. Too much should not be made of the fact that Paul uses the Greek word ἄλλον (as opposed to ἕτερον) here when he says that 'another Jesus' had been preached among them. It is well known that the classical distinction between the two terms (the former meaning 'another of the *same* kind' and the latter 'another of a different kind') has broken down by the time that the New Testament documents were written. Subtlety of grammatical distinction does not resolve the issue, especially when Paul on occasion uses the two Greek words interchangeably (as in 1 Cor. 12.9-10 and Gal. 1.6-7).

Paul counters his opponents in 11.2-3 with an evocative use of the marriage-betrothal metaphor, mixing it with an allusion from Genesis 3 to the deceit of Eve by the serpent in the Garden of Eden. In effect this is to portray the Corinthians as a betrothed woman who is in danger of being wooed away from the eagerly-awaited marriage to her husband. This powerful image is designed to shame the church into repenting of its spiritual adultery and returning to the truth of her marriage to Christ (which is to be consummated at the parousia?). At the same time, it has

the additional benefit of placing Paul in the traditional role
of a Jewish father responsible for safe-guarding the purity of
his daughter-bride (the Corinthian church) so that she might
be acceptable to her husband-to-be (Jesus Christ). The use of
such an emotive image stands as testimony to the seriousness with which Paul viewed the situation at Corinth. Suffice
it to say that Paul saw the challenge to the gospel message
he proclaimed as striking right at the heart of his apostolic
calling. To deny the gospel Paul preached was to deny his
apostleship, and to deny his apostleship was to deny the Lord
who had called him into service.

Having summarized some of the main features of the controversy between the Corinthian opponents and Paul, we are
now in a position to address some of the most exciting new
developments in Pauline studies. There are several important areas of research which find the issue of Paul's apostolic
ministry at their heart. Indeed, the Corinthian correspondence in general, and 2 Corinthians 10–13 in particular,
have figured prominently in recent scholarly discussion with
the complex question of Paul's apostleship being a focal
point. There is space to introduce two such areas here, both
of which might be described as methodological approaches to
addressing the question of how Paul perceived, and exercised, his apostleship among the Corinthian congregation for
which he felt largely responsible.

Methodological Approaches to Paul's Apostleship

Sociological Studies of the Corinthian Epistles
The Corinthian epistles have been the subject of particular
scholarly interest by those keen to apply to them insights
drawn from sociology. Several studies use insights drawn
from Max Weber's pioneering work in sociology as a platform
upon which to analyse Paul's letters—so much so that sociological studies of the Pauline churches based upon his
correspondence with them have become one of the most
significant growth-industries of research, particularly in the
1970s and 1980s. A seminal figure in this regard has been
Gerd Theissen, whose most significant articles on the
Corinthian situation have been brought together under the
title *The Social Setting of Pauline Christianity* (1982)

(Theissen is here building upon his earlier study from 1978 which posits an analysis of the Jesus movement based upon a sociological theory of *conflict*. In contrast, Theissen asserts, the setting of Pauline Christianity in Hellenism is based upon a sociological theory of *integration*). Theissen argues, quite reasonably, that the Corinthian conflicts are rooted in the social and economic settings of the church and that Paul is attempting to bring what he describes as a 'love-patriarchialism' to bear in the situation. A recognition of the household nature of the early Christian congregations lies at the heart of much of Theissen's work and it has given rise to a number of other significant studies which follow this approach. One of the most accessible books on this subject is Robert Banks's *Paul's Idea of Community: The Early House Churches in their Historical Setting* (1980), which stresses the sociological similarities between churches and households. In contrast, one of Banks's students, S.C. Barton (1986) turns his arguments around somewhat by attempting to show the sociological boundaries between the two. Barton identifies two passages (1 Cor. 11.17-34 and 14.33b-36) in which Paul appears to be in conflict with the Corinthians over precisely where the line of division between church and home is to be drawn. Several other important studies are also worth mentioning.

J.H. Schütz (1975) applies sociological definitions of power, authority and legitimacy to a number of Pauline passages (including 2 Cor. 2.14–7.4 and 10–13). Schütz defines the relationship between the three concepts, arguing that authority is best viewed as concerned with the interpretation of power, while legitimacy is best viewed as concerned with the interpretation of authority. Similarly, B. Holmberg (1978) assesses the distribution of power and the structures of authority which were contained in churches associated with Paul's ministry; W.A. Meeks (1983) seeks to set Paul's ministry within the social setting of an urban city in the ancient world; F. Watson (1986) addresses the crucial question of Jewish–Gentile relationships in Paul's thought from a sociological perspective; J.K. Chow (1992) analyses the Corinthian correspondence against the Hellenistic idea of patronage; F.W. Danker (1989) stresses the Graeco-Roman

system of benefaction as a backdrop against which to view
2 Corinthians, especially in light of the Imperial policy of
Nero, Emperor at the time Paul was writing the letter; and
N.R. Petersen (1985) and D.B. Martin (1990) both attempt to
give due consideration to the question of how Paul tackles
the complicated issue of slavery within the ancient world.
One of the most important insights that arises out of such
sociological approaches to Paul's life and ministry is the
recognition that his disagreements with opponents cannot be
viewed simply as a theological controversy or a theoretical
christological dispute alone, for, as B. Holmberg remarks
(1978, p. 202), there is 'a continuous dialectic between ideas
and social structures'.

The question of Paul's apostleship has been one of the
areas most illuminated by such an approach, mainly because
so much of the matter understandably revolves around questions which are essentially sociological in nature, such as
power and authority, conflict and the resolution of disputes.
The manner in which Paul jealously defended attacks upon
his apostleship, particularly in 2 Corinthians 10–13, has led
some to question his pastoral gifts and suitability as a church
leader. For example, one recent interpreter, G. Shaw (1983),
has gone so far as to suggest that Paul abused the power he
had as an apostle, engaging in self-righteous attacks on his
opponents which contradicted his dubious claim to promote
Christian freedom. In effect, Paul is taken to be extremely
manipulative in how he deals with the congregation in
Corinth, browbeating them about their responsibility with
regard to the collection and never failing to remind them of
their indebtedness to him as the one responsible for bringing
them to faith in Christ. At first glance there is something to
commend such a reading of Paul, despite the fact that it is
motivated by what F. Young (in her review of G. Shaw's *The
Cost of Authority* contained in *Theology* [September 1983],
p. 380) describes as a 'thorough-going hermeneutic of moral
suspicion'. However, other recent interpreters of Paul have
questioned the extent to which Paul invokes his authority *as
an apostle* when dealing with congregations with which he is
associated. For example, E. Best (1986) puts forward the
interesting suggestion that Paul did not use his apostleship

as a basis upon which to exhort or chastise his converts; instead he used his authority over them as a father-figure, the founder of their congregation(s). Where Paul *did* use his position as an apostle, Best continues, is in his relationships with other church leaders. This is to approach the idea of Paul's apostolic authority from a different direction. Moreover, a more rigorous attention to the complexities of social interaction reveals an infinitely more complex picture than some of the wholly negative assessments of Paul that are on offer. One can hardly blame *all* of the problems of Corinth on the irascible nature of Paul himself.

In a more balanced study, P. Marshall (1987) addresses why it is that Paul's rivals in Corinth are presented in such negative terms. Marshall notes that Paul deliberately avoids mentioning his opponents by name or addressing them directly. This, he suggests, is in conformity to a standard rhetorical style within the Hellenistic world and lends itself to a caricature of his rivals. This fine study by Marshall also stresses how Paul deliberately portrays himself in his quarrel with the Corinthian opponents as a socially disadvantaged person, an object of shame and ridicule. He points to a number of passages (including 2 Cor. 4.8-9; 6.4-10 and 11.23-33), in which Paul presents himself as one who experienced social shame. He does this, so Marshall argues, as a means of demonstrating the true nature of his apostleship; it is to be evaluated on the basis of failure and weakness, not by strength and power which would be to apply human standards, rather than God's, to the situation.

Rhetorical Studies of 2 Corinthians
A second area of fruitful investigation has been the study of the use of classical rhetorical styles and forms by which Paul defends his apostleship. If sociological studies of 1 and 2 Corinthians have been the way forward for the Corinthian correspondence in general, then rhetorical-critical studies have been the single most important advance for interpreting 2 Corinthians in particular. It has even been suggested that long-debated questions about the unity of the epistle as a whole can perhaps be solved by an appeal to how the ancients structured rhetorical arguments. Thus F. Young and D.F. Ford (1987) argue that the canonical 2 Corinthians

falls into four sections and conforms to the rhetorical conventions laid down centuries earlier by such Greek and Latin
theorists as Aristotle and Quintilian. The result of such a
suggestion is that the oft-asserted incompatibility of chs.
1–9 and 10–13 no longer stands up to scrutiny; the final four
chapters simply stand as the concluding section of Paul's
rhetorical argument, recapitulating the ideas contained in
the body of the epistle.

The last two decades have witnessed a veritable explosion
of monographs and articles on rhetorical criticism, particularly as it relates to 2 Corinthians 10–13. Paul's boasting in
2 Corinthians 10–13 has been compared to other contemporary examples of Hellenistic rhetoric. Special attention
has been given by a number of scholars to Paul's use of
such formal categories as abbreviation, irony, parody, self-
praise, sarcasm, invective and the cultivation of good will
(*benevolentia*) in his dealings with the Corinthian rivals.

Not surprisingly, particular passages from 2 Corinthians
10–13 have been focal points of attention in such endeavours,
notably the section on boasting contained in 10.13-18.
Similarly, the so-called 'foolish discourse' of 11.16–12.10 has
received much scholarly attention. In addition, the prominent
use that Paul makes of diatribe, in which he quotes the words
and ideas of the Corinthians themselves within his arguments, has also been the subject of special note. The connection between sociological analyses of how power and
authority were seen to operate within the Pauline churches
can be closely aligned with rhetorical-critical approaches to
the Corinthian letters, particularly 2 Corinthians. A good
example of this is the highly creative study by J.A. Crafton
(1991).

Essentially Crafton builds upon those who have argued
that the essence of the debate between Paul and his
Corinthian opponents concerns the difference between
authority and legitimacy. However, he grounds his interpretation in the specialized branch of rhetorical-criticism known
as dramatistic analysis (as pioneered by the influential
rhetorician Kenneth Burke). When applied to 2 Corinthians
this approach suggests that a distinction needs to be drawn
between apostleship as conceived in terms of *agency* and

apostleship as conceived in terms of agent. The Corinthian opponents of Paul, so Crafton suggests, viewed apostleship primarily in terms of an agent-perspective, whereas Paul's conception was of it in terms of agency (with God *himself* being the operative agent behind the activity of his appointed apostles). An interpretative approach such as this has much to offer, crucially dependent though it is upon a particular decision about the partition of 2 Corinthians, as well as operating with a determined chronological reconstruction. Crafton divides the canonical epistle into four main letters and bases his assessment upon the assumption that the opponents Paul is addressing in 2 Corinthians have arrived on the scene after the sending of 1 Corinthians. He also takes Paul to have visited Corinth shortly after his first letter to them in which he addresses the arrival of the opponents. The four letters Crafton identifies are, in order of composition and sending: (1) The Letter of Initial Response (2.14–6.13 and 7.2-4); (2) The Letter of Attack (10.1–13.13); (3) The Letter of Reconciliation (1.3–2.13 and 7.5-16); (4) The Letters of the Collection (chs. 8–9). Crafton is concerned primarily with the first three of these letters and he argues that they represent various stages in Paul's dealings with the Corinthians, each exhibiting slightly different ways of presenting the opposition between agent and agency depending upon Paul's rhetorical aim. The awkward passage of 2 Cor. 6.14–7.1 is deemed by Crafton to be an interpolation and does not figure in his discussion. Moreover, chs. 8–9 are taken to reflect a calmer period in Paul's relationship with the Corinthians and thus were probably written after the remainder of the material contained in the canonical letter; hence, they do not figure prominently in his discussion either.

There is much that such a dramatistic analysis provides in unlocking some of the vexing problems of 2 Corinthians. For example, it does offer an explanation for the puzzling fluctuation between the use of first-person language and second-person language within the document as a whole. Crafton suggests that second-person language is employed when the focus is on presenting the agency model of apostleship (as in 2.14–6.13 and 7.2-4); however, first-person language becomes

necessary when Paul is presenting himself as a counter-
agent (as in 10.1–13.13). The approach adopted by Crafton
also sheds light upon key passages which deal with the
nature of apostleship and the way in which Paul chooses to
address the Corinthians in his dispute with them over the
matter. For example, the interpretation of a passage such as
2 Cor. 3.12-18 is assisted by this dramatistic approach
insofar as an understanding of apostolic ministry focusing
upon the agent inevitably becomes associated with a 'veiled'
ministry (in which the human *agent* gets in the way of divine
manifestation). On the other hand, an understanding of
ministry focusing upon the *agency* of an apostle is associated
with an 'unveiled' ministry (in which the divine encounter
can take place unhindered).

A careful analysis of various rhetorical techniques has
allowed fresh understandings of the subtlety of Paul's arguments to be recognized; this has in turn challenged some of
the conventional understandings of Paul's opponents and the
nature of their arguments. For example, C. Forbes (1986,
p. 17) argues that C.K. Barrett's distinction between the
'Judaizing apostles' and the 'super-apostles' of 11.5 and 12.11
is rendered superfluous when the rhetorical forms are properly understood. Rhetorical approaches have also been
employed in recent attempts to address complex questions
about the unity of 2 Corinthians and to challenge the validity
of partition theories of the letter. This has been particularly
useful in analyzing 2 Cor. 1.1-8.24 where the rhetorical
structure of an argument (running from 1.1–2.13 and 7.5-24)
appears to be broken up by an intervening passage, namely
2 Cor. 2.14–7.4. The study of rhetorical style is often closely
associated with attempts to detect within Paul's letters to the
Corinthians a chiastic structure to his argument.

In conclusion, Paul's understanding of his apostolic
ministry is central to a study of 2 Corinthians. Not only does
the topic give us a window through which to view the nature
of the controversy that Paul is embroiled in at Corinth, but it
has also prompted significant investigations into Paul's
rhetorical style and invited many important sociological
studies of the congregation there. Nowhere can this integration of approach be seen more clearly than in the most recent

study of Ben Witherington (1995) which is a full-bodied attempt to interpret the Corinthian letters by giving due recognition to the various sociological and rhetorical tools at the disposal of modern scholarship. Such interdisciplinary approaches point the way of the future and promise that the Corinthian epistles, perhaps more than any other section of the New Testament, will continue to be at the forefront of historical-critical discussion as we enter the third millennium.

Suggestions for Further Reading

On Paul's Apostolic Authority

P.W. Barnett, 'Apostle', in G.F. Hawthorne, R.P. Martin and D.G. Reid (eds.), *Dictionary of Paul and his Letters* (Leicester: Inter-Varsity Press, 1993), pp. 45-51.

C.K. Barrett, *The Signs of an Apostle* (London: Epworth Press, 1970).

—'Shaliah and Apostle', in E. Bammel, C.K. Barrett and W.D. Davies (eds.), *Donum Gentilicium: New Testament Studies in Honour of David Daube* (Oxford: Clarendon Press, 1978), pp. 88-102.

—'Boasting (καυχᾶσθαι, κτλ.) in the Pauline Epistles', in A. Vanhoye (ed.), *L'Apôtre Paul: Personnalité, style et conception du ministère* (Leuven: Leuven University Press, 1986), pp. 363-68.

L.L. Belleville, 'Gospel and Kerygma in 2 Corinthians', in L.A. Jervis and P. Richardson (eds.), *Gospel in Paul: Studies on Corinthians, Galatians and Romans for Richard N. Longenecker* (JSNTSup, 108; Sheffield: Sheffield Academic Press, 1994), pp. 134-64.

E. Best, 'Paul's Apostolic Authority—?', *JSNT* 27 (1986), pp. 3-25.

D.A. Black, *Paul, Apostle of Weakness: Astheneia and its Cognates in the Pauline Literature* (New York: Peter Lang, 1984).

N.A. Dahl, *Studies in Paul: Theology for the Early Christian Mission* (Minneapolis: Augsburg, 1977).

G.D. Fee, ' "Another Gospel which you Did not Embrace": 2 Corinthians 11.4 and the Theology of 1 and 2 Corinthians', in L.A. Jervis and P. Richardson (eds.), *Gospel in Paul: Studies on Corinthians, Galatians and Romans for Richard N. Longenecker* (JSNTSup, 108; Sheffield: Sheffield Academic Press, 1994), pp. 111-33.

V.P. Furnish, 'Paul the MARTUS', in P.E. Devenish and G.L. Goodwin (eds.), *Witness and Existence: Essays in Honor of Schubert M. Ogden* (Chicago: University of Chicago Press, 1989), pp. 73-88.

S.J. Hafemann, ' "Self-Commendation" and Apostolic Legitimacy in 2 Corinthians: A Pauline Dialectic?', *NTS* 36 (1990), pp. 66-88.

R.P. Martin, 'The Setting of 2 Corinthians', *TynBul* 37 (1986), pp. 3-19.

S.C. Mott, 'The Power of Giving and Receiving: Reciprocity in Hellenistic Benevolence', in G.F. Hawthorne (ed.), *Current Issues in Biblical and Patristic Interpretation: Studies in Honor of Merrill C. Tenney* (Grand Rapids: Eerdmans, 1975), pp. 60-72.

J. Murphy-O'Connor, 'Another Jesus (2 Cor. 11.4)', *RB* 97 (1990), pp. 238-51.

W. Schmithals, *The Office of the Apostle in the Early Church* (Nashville: Abingdon Press, 1969).

R. Schnackenburg, 'Apostles before and during Paul's Time', in W.W. Gasque and R.P. Martin (eds.), *Apostolic History and the Gospel: Essays Presented to F.F. Bruce* (Exeter: Paternoster Press, 1970), pp. 287-303.

G. Shaw, *The Cost of Authority: Manipulation and Freedom in the New Testament* (London: SCM Press, 1983).

M.E. Thrall, 'Christ Crucified or Second Adam? A Christological Debate between Paul and the Corinthians', in B. Lindars and S. Smalley (eds.), *Christ and Spirit in the New Testament: Essays in Honour of C.F.D. Moule* (Cambridge: Cambridge University Press, 1973), pp. 143-56.

D. Wenham, '2 Corinthians 1.17,18. Echo of a Dominical Logion', *NovT* 28 (1986), pp. 271-79.

On the Letters of Commendation (2 Cor. 3.1)

W. Baird, 'Letters of Recommendation: A Study of II Corinthians 3.1-3', *JBL* 80 (1961), pp. 166-72.

C.J.A. Hickling, 'The Sequence of Thought in II Corinthians, Chapter Three', *NTS* 21 (1975), pp. 380-95.

On Sociological Studies of the Corinthian Correspondence

R. Banks, *Paul's Idea of Community: The Early House Churches in their Historical Setting* (Exeter: Paternoster Press, 1980).

S.C. Barton, 'Paul's Sense of Place: An Anthropological Approach to Community Formation in Corinth', *NTS* 32 (1986), pp. 225-46.

—'Social-Scientific Approaches to Paul', in G.F Hawthorne, R.P. Martin and D.G. Reid (eds.), *Dictionary of Paul and his Letters* (Leicester: Inter-Varsity Press, 1993), pp. 892-900.

J.K. Chow, *Patronage and Power: A Study of Social Networks in Corinth* (JSNTSup, 75; Sheffield: JSOT Press, 1992).

A.J. Dewey, 'A Matter of Honor: A Socio-Historical Analysis of 2 Corinthians 10', *HTR* 78 (1985), pp. 209-17.

B. Holmberg, *Sociology and the New Testament* (Minneapolis: Augsburg–Fortress, 1990).

D.B. Martin, *Slavery as Salvation: The Metaphor of Slavery in Pauline Christianity* (London: Yale University Press, 1990).

N.R. Petersen, *Rediscovering Paul: Philemon and the Sociology of Paul's Narrative World* (Philadelphia: Fortess Press, 1985).

R. Scroggs, 'The Sociological Interpretation of the New Testament: The Present State of Research', *NTS* 26 (1980), pp. 164-79.

D. Tidball, 'Social Setting of Mission Churches', in G.F Hawthorne, R.P. Martin and D.G Reid (eds.), *Dictionary of Paul and his Letters* (Leicester: Inter-Varsity Press, 1993), pp. 883-92.

On Rhetorical Studies of the Corinthian Correspondence

H.D. Betz, *Der Apostel Paulus und die sokratische Tradition: Eine exegetische Untersuchung zu seiner 'Apologie' 2 Kor 10–13* (BHT, 45; Tübingen: J.C.B. Mohr, 1972).

—'The Problem of Rhetoric and Theology according to the Apostle Paul', in A. Vanhoye (ed.), *L'Apôtre Paul: Personnalité, style et conception du ministère* (Leuven: Leuven University Press, 1986), pp. 16-48.

T. Callan, 'Competition and Boasting: Toward a Psychological Portrait of Paul', *JRelS* 13 (1986), pp. 27-51.

C. Forbes, 'Comparison, Self-Praise and Irony: Paul's Boasting and the Conventions of Hellenistic Rhetoric', *NTS* 32 (1986), pp. 1-30.

S.B. Heiny, '2 Corinthians 2.14–4.6. The Motive for Metaphor', in K.H. Richards (ed.), *Society of Biblical Literature 1987 Seminar Papers* (Atlanta: Scholars Press, 1987), pp. 1-22.

G. Holland, 'Speaking Like a Fool: Irony in 2 Corinthians 10-13', in S.E. Porter and T.H. Olbricht (eds.), *Rhetoric and the New Testament: Essays from the 1992 Heidelberg Conference* (JSNTSup, 90; Sheffield: JSOT Press, 1993), pp. 250-64.

F.W. Hughes, 'The Rhetoric of Reconciliation: 2 Corinthians 1.1–2.13 and 7.5–8.24', in D.F. Watson (ed.), *Persuasive Artistry: Studies in New Testament Rhetoric in Honor of George A. Kennedy* (JSNTSup, 50; Sheffield: JSOT Press, 1991), pp. 246-61.

E.A. Judge, 'Paul's Boasting in Relation to Contemporary Professional Practice', *ABR* 16 (1968), pp. 37-50.

P. Marshall, 'Invective: Paul and his Enemies in Corinth', in E.W. Conrad and E.G. Newing (eds.), *Perspectives on Language and Text: Essays and Poems in Honor of Francis I. Andersen's Sixtieth Birthday* (Winona Lake, IN: Eisenbrauns, 1987), pp. 359-73.

M.M. Mitchell, 'Rhetorical Shorthand in Pauline Argumentation: The Functions of "The Gospel" in the Corinthian Correspondence', in L.A. Jervis and P. Richardson (eds.), *Gospel in Paul: Studies on Corinthians, Galatians and Romans for Richard N. Longenecker* (JSNTSup, 108; Sheffield: Sheffield Academic Press, 1994), pp. 63-88.

K. Plank, *Paul and the Irony of Affliction* (SBLSS; Atlanta: Scholars Press, 1987).

J.P. Sampley, 'Paul, his Opponents in 2 Corinthians 10-13, and the Rhetorical Handbooks', in J. Neusner, P. Borgen, E.S. Frerichs and R. Horsley (eds.), *The Social World of Formative Christianity and Judaism: In Tribute to Howard Clark Kee* (Philadelphia: Fortress Press, 1988), pp. 162-77.

A.B. Spencer, 'The Wise Fool (and the Foolish Wise): A Study of Irony in Paul', *NovT* 23 (1981), pp. 349-60.

S.H. Travis, 'Paul's Boasting in 2 Corinthians 10–12', in *SE VI* (Texte und Untersuchungen zür Geschichte der altchristlichen Literatur; Band 112; ed. E.A. Livingstone; Berlin: Akademie-Verlag, 1973), pp. 527-32.

B. Witherington, III, *Conflict and Community in Corinth: A Socio-Rhetorical Commentary on 1 and 2 Corinthians* (Grand Rapids: Eerdmans, 1995).

J. Zmijewski, *Der Stil der paulinische 'Narrenrede': Analyse der Sprachgestaltung in 2 Kor 11.1-12.10 als Beitrag zur Methodik von Stiluntersuchungen neutestamentlicher Texte* (BBB, 52; Cologne: Peter Hanstein, 1978).

4

MOSES, GLORY
AND THE NEW COVENANT

Most agree that 2 Corinthians 1–4 is part of an extended apologetic section in which Paul aggressively defends his apostleship. A variety of structural analyses of the section have been put forward in support of this suggestion, particularly of 2.14–4.6, which is commonly regarded as a single unit within the apology. 2 Corinthians 3 has often been identified as holding a central position within these studies, and for this reason, among others, its purpose within Paul's argument has been the subject of much interest. For example, J. Murphy-O'Connor (1986), as part of his suggestion that Paul is confronting both πνευματικοί and Judaizers in Corinth, argues that 3.7-18 is deliberately inserted by the apostle into the letter between two other apologetic sections, namely 2.14–3.6 and 4.1-6. This, so Murphy-O'Connor continues, Paul does in order to drive a wedge between the two factions he is confronting and to try and convince the πνευματικοί to disregard the troublesome intruders from Jerusalem (the Judaizers).

Moreover, 3.1-18 has become one of the most discussed passages in the whole of the Pauline corpus by virtue of the tantalyzing allusions to Moses and the new covenant, along with the related juxtaposition of the spirit and the letter, which are contained within the verses. However, the formal antithesis between the spirit and the letter is infrequent within the New Testament, occurring only here in 2 Cor. 3.6, and in Rom. 2.29 and 7.6. The highly structured contrast in

3.6 between the letter of the Mosaic law (which leads to death) and the freedom of the Spirit (which leads to life) has led to extensive discussion of Paul's hermeneutical method and its implications for his understanding of the relationship between Christianity and Judaism as religious faiths (E. Käsemann [1971, pp. 138-66] offers a classic study along these lines). Yet things are not as straightforward as such a simple contrast implies and there are indications within the text of 2 Corinthians 3 itself which cast doubt upon it. To illustrate: R.B. Hays (1989, pp. 130-31, 151) suggests that a distinction needs to be made between 'letter' (γράμμα) and 'writing' (γράφη) in 2 Cor. 3.6. He suggests that grámma is better translated as 'that which is inscribed', and links back to 3.3. This means that the focus of the contrast between the old and the new covenants is not on them as texts, and certainly not on the way that texts are interpreted within them. Rather, the contrast is between a written code of life and a Spirit-empowered code of life. Thus, Hays rightly warns (p. 222) against 'the danger of a Christian misreading of the gramma/pneuma polarity as a distinction between Judaism and Christianity'. Suffice it to say, investigations into Paul's attitudes to the Mosaic law are exceedingly complex and represent perhaps the single most significant development in Pauline studies in the past twenty years. We must be very careful not to read into 2 Cor. 3.1-18 a contrast between Judaism and Christianity that Paul did not intend and which is based on our own preconceived ideas about the relationship of the two faiths. It is important to remember that the basic purpose of 2.14–4.6 is as an apology for Paul's apostleship in particular, and for Christian ministry in general. Although the text of 2.14–4.6 invites careful attention to the use to which Paul puts Scripture citations, the passage is not designed as a programmatic statement about how Christian believers should interpret the writings of the Old Testament. This means that Paul's discussion is *not* intended as a polemic against Judaism as a whole, wherein the superiority of the Christian reading of Scripture is asserted. Rather, the focus of the letter-spirit contrast is on how life is to be lived, and service rendered, within the bounds of the two respective covenants.

The reliance upon Exod. 34.29-35 in these verses is evident
and affords one of the best opportunities to examine how
Paul uses Old Testament Scripture in the course of his apostolic apology. It is this feature of the passage which will be
the primary concern in the discussion here. The exploration
of the subject will begin by considering the question of the
nature of 2 Corinthians 3 as a midrash, and then moving on
to address five particular issues that arise from the text
itself.

A Christian Midrash?

2 Cor. 3.7-18 has often been described as a Christian
midrash on Exodus 34, perhaps drawing on conventional
Jewish interpretations of the text. Some have suggested that
an extended midrash of Exod. 34.28-35 was circulating
among the Jewish Christian opponents in Corinth, and that
Paul demonstrates his familiarity with this tradition when
he pens 2 Cor. 3.7, 12-18. However, the traditions about
Moses (and the glory which he manifests in his countenance
as a result of his encounter with God on Mount Sinai) are
varied and diffuse and it is impossible to prove that Paul was
responding to one particular interpretation or another. It is
much more likely that Paul is interweaving extra-biblical
traditions and his own distinctive interpretations in the
course of his letter to the Corinthian church. Moreover, the
wider world of Hellenism may also be partly responsible for
Paul's description of the transfiguration of Moses' face as
there is a long tradition of such an idea in Greek literature.
Thus, F.W. Danker (1989, p. 56) cites as a parallel the story
of the visage of Achilles being transformed under the power
of the goddess Athena in *Iliad* 18.203-206.

That Paul deviates from the text of both the LXX and the MT
in his citation of Exodus 34 has long been noted. So too has
the fact that in 3.7 and 3.13 he freely inserts motifs not
explicitly found in the Old Testament story. Three such
insertions are made:

1.   The effect that Moses' appearance had upon the
     people of Israel is noted: 'the Israelites could not bear
     to look at his face because of its brightness' (3.7).

2. The transitory nature of the glory of his face is described: 'fading as it was' (3.7).

3. The reason for Moses veiling himself is given: 'so that the Israelites might not see the end of the fading splendour' (3.13).

W.C. Van Unnik (1963) notes these additions and offers a highly creative interpretation of the word 'bold' (παρρησία) in 3.12 as a partial explanation for their insertion. He suggests that the term is to be associated with Semitic ideas of freedom of speech, the authority to speak 'openly and in public'. Each of the three insertions has been intensively debated, mainly because of the implications that they have for determining Paul's attitude toward his native Judaism now that he has committed himself to Jesus Christ. One prime focal point within such scholarly debate has been the essential meaning of the phrase translated in the RSV as 'fading' (τὴν καταργουμένην) in 3.7. How one interprets the sense of the verb (and the participles built on it contained in 3.11 and 3.13!) can make a great deal of theological difference. If we take the verb καταργεῖν to mean 'to fade', then it is but one small step to assert the inferiority of the Mosaic law and Judaism as judged over against the permanence of the new covenant in Christ. If unchecked this line of interpretation can lead to a wholly negative assessment of Judaism, something which, as was noted above, Paul cannot be assumed to have intended here. On the other hand, if the verb is translated as 'to pass away' or 'to nullify' or 'to abrogate', a more productive interpretative possibility arises, namely a continuity between the old and the new covenants. This means that the old covenant is not something inherently flawed, or wrong-headed, and doomed to fade by its very nature. Rather, it is simply a covenant which has been superseded by the new covenant in Christ.

Explanations for the Halting Style of Argument in 3.1–4.6

It is not immediately apparent why it is that Paul comes to include the story of Moses and the veiling of his glory within his argument of 3.1–4.6. The transitions from 3.3 to 3.4 and

from 3.11 to 3.12-18 seem rough and unclear, especially
given that 3.1-3 opens the section with a seemingly unrelated
discussion of 'letters of recommendation' which Paul's opponents in Corinth apparently prized so much. When this is
added to the fact that 3.12-18 might conceivably be taken to
interrupt the flow of thought running between 3.1-11 and
4.1-6, one immediately begins to see some of the special problems raised by this section of 2 Corinthians. Given such
difficulties, it is hardly surprising that some have suggested
that Paul picks up the Moses/new covenant motif directly
from his Corinthian opponents, reworking it to fit his critique
of them. An important result of such a suggestion is that the
apostle's interaction with *their* ideas is held responsible, at
least in part, for the stop-and-start character of the flow of
Paul's argument. However, despite the advantages this
suggestion provides in terms of explaining the awkward
transitions of thought in the passage, it rests on a wholly
hypothetical reconstruction of the Corinthians' thought and
is therefore fraught with its own methodological problems.
Consequently it has not commanded widespread acceptance.

Other attempts at integrating 3.12-18 within the thought
of 3.1-11 and 4.1-6 have also been put forward. For example,
J.A. Fitzmyer (1983) attempts to trace a free-flowing association of ideas throughout chs. 3–4, arriving at a conclusion
which does account for some of the abrupt transitions in the
material. Similarly, M. Hooker (1990), who describes
2 Corinthians 3 as a 'somewhat muddled metaphor' (p. 9),
suggests that there is a logical *non sequitur* in Paul's thought
as he moves from 3.7-11 to 3.12-18, the former section being
primarily concerned with contrast between the ministry of
the old covenant and the ministry of the new and the latter
section being concerned with the significance of the veil. As
she says (p. 143):

> Paul is using the idea of glory in two different ways in the two
> paragraphs, and we shall misunderstand him completely if we try
> to combine the two arguments.

In contrast, J. Lambrecht (1983) does not feel that Paul's
argument rests on anything as haphazard, or as potentially
misleading, as the free association of ideas, or the inexplic-
able shift in meaning of key terms. He offers instead a rather

full chiastic outline of 2.14–4.6 which he feels demonstrates the logical flow of the argument and shows the connections of thought throughout the passage. On the other hand, C.K. Stockhausen (1989) is critical of attempts to interpret 2 Cor. 3.1–4.6 based solely upon what is in effect a study of the social world of Paul and his opponents. Instead she proposes to approach the section by means of a close attention to the *theological* argument that is conducted within it. A literary (as opposed to a sociological) basis of investigation is set up within her study, one of the most thorough available on this section of 2 Corinthians. Crucial to Stockhausen's argument are the textual interrelationships between the various Old Testament passages which Paul cites or alludes to in his discussion of Moses and the new covenant. The text is divided into three sections (3.1-6; 3.7-18; 4.1-6), and once we recognize the exegetical techniques which Paul employs, we can see that the argument readily flows from one section to the next. She suggests that Paul uses several standard methods of Jewish exegesis in the course of his discussion in these chapters, including the association of ideas by means of key 'hook-words'. Paul's exegetical skills are evident in 2 Cor. 3.1–4.6 and he clearly demonstrates how those skills could be put into practice in composing an apology for his ministry.

The Letters of Recommendation and the New Covenant Written on Human Hearts

What is the link between the 'letters of recommendation' (3.1) and the description of the Moses/new covenant motif which follows (3.7, 12-18)? The connection is by no means immediately obvious. Some have suggested that 2 Cor. 3.3b serves as an important bridge of thought between the two ideas. Here Paul adapts the image of the Corinthians as *his* letter of recommendation and shifts to new covenant imagery, probably under the guiding influence of Jer. 31.33 (MT) where the new covenant is said to be 'written on human hearts'. That Christ has established a *new* covenant seems to be an essential feature of Pauline theology, as the use in 3.6 of the phrase 'the new covenant' (= καινὴ διαθήκη), which is drawn from Jer. 31.31, indicates. However, not all accept this interpretation of 3.3b. For example, L.L. Belleville (1991, pp. 146-47) disagrees, arguing that it has the effect of reducing 3.7-18 to a mere excursus on the new covenant idea.

A collage of Old Testament allusions and images are presented by the apostle in the course of his argument. For example, allusions to the stone tablets upon which the Spirit of God engraved the Mosaic Law (Exod. 31.18 and Deut. 9.10-11) are contained in 2 Cor. 3.3. Similarly, it is highly probable that Ezek. 11.19 and 36.26-27 are also in Paul's mind given the unusual phrase 'hearts of flesh' (καρδίαις σαρκίναις) which he uses in 3.3. Yet the only explicit citation from the Old Testament contained in 3.1–4.6 occurs in 3.16 where Paul slightly paraphrases Exod. 34.34 and adds his own interpretative comment in the succeeding verse. This exegetical addition culminates in a resounding declaration of 'freedom' (ἐλευθερία), a fitting word to sum up what the new covenant means for Christian believers.

Moses and Paul as Ministers of God's Covenant

If Jeremiah's image of a new covenant underlies 2 Cor. 3.1-3 and sets in motion the general comparison of Paul's apostolic ministry with that of his opponents, we find an even more explicit juxtaposition of the two in 3.6. Here Paul combines the metaphor of written documents (or engraved tablets) with a declaration of his worthiness to minister as an apostle of Jesus Christ.

In light of the many Old Testament passages alluded to in 2 Corinthians, W. Lane (1982) has put forward the suggestion that the idea of the new covenant in Christ lies at the heart of the controversy that Paul has with the Corinthian church. He argues that 2 Cor. 3.1–7.1 follows the pattern of an Old Testament covenant lawsuit and that Paul views his task as that of a prophetic figure (modelled after Isa. 49.1-13) who is responsible for reconciling the wayward Corinthians with their sovereign God. Thus, to follow the structural pattern of a covenant lawsuit, Lane argues that 3.1-5.19 represents a response to charges against a royal messenger; 5.20-21 represents the offended sovereign; 6.14-18 represents the warning against idolatry; and 7.1 represents the blessing

4. *Moses, Glory and the New Covenant*   63

promised by God to the faithful. In pursuing this line of
interpretation, Lane goes so far as to suggest that Paul
consciously presents himself as a second Moses, a new leader
for the renewed covenant community: 'As Moses was preemi-
nently the mediator and prophet of the Old Covenant, Paul is
the mediator and prophet of the New Covenant' (p. 8). The
interesting parallel in 3.5 between the calling of Moses and
the calling of Paul supports such an interpretation. The
parallel revolves around the use of the word 'worthiness': 'our
worthiness is from God' (ἡ ἱκανότης ἡμῶν ἐκ τοῦ θεοῦ). The
point here is that a similar expression is used by Moses in
Exod. 4.10 when he encounters the Lord in the burning bush
and receives his calling. Moses has grave doubts about his
ability to serve as God's prophet and says (Exod. 4.10): 'Lord,
I am not worthy' (κύριε οὐχ ἱκανός εἰμι). It is easy to understand how one might see in 2 Cor. 3.5-7 an allusion to this
Old Testament story where Moses is invoked by Paul.
Neither should we fail to note that the two are being
contrasted as religious leaders responsible for establishing
their respective covenants between God and the people of
Israel. At the same time, Moses and Paul are united insofar
as they both find that their worthiness for the task at hand
comes to them as a gift from God Himself.

However, such a formalized covenantal interpretation as
Lane suggests, as intriguing as it may be, falters because it
fails to take into account the epistolary nature of
2 Corinthians as a whole and because 2 Corinthians 3 does
not really conform to the formal pattern of such a covenantal
lawsuit. Nevertheless, it seems probable that to some degree
Paul does compare his role as a minister of the covenant to
that of Moses, despite the fact that elsewhere (notably in
Rom. 10.6-7 and possibly Rom. 5.14?) it is arguably the Lord
Jesus Christ rather than himself whom Paul compares to
Moses. There may be something of a parallel here to the way
in which the Teacher of Righteousness is similarly presented
as a new Moses figure in a number of documents from
Qumran. It has even been argued, rather implausibly, that
in 2 Cor. 3.6 Paul is reacting to the Essene understanding of
the 'new covenant'.

However, we should not think that it is only the contrast

between himself and Moses (as ministers of their respective covenants) which Paul wishes to stress within 2 Corinthians 3. It is clear that Paul's argument in the chapter also carries with it an implied contrast between the Christians (as members of the new covenant) and the people of Israel (as members of the old covenant). As N.T. Wright (1991) puts it:

> the main contrast in the passage is not that between Paul and Moses, but that between the Christians - even those in Corinth!— and the Israelites, both of Moses' day and of Paul's (p. 180).

The Veil over Moses' Face

Why does Paul say that Moses hid his face with a veil (2 Cor. 3.13)? What is the significance of this unusual image? In part the answer to these questions is dependent upon our recognizing that Paul uses the metaphor of the veil in two slightly different ways in 3.7-16 and that a subtle, but all-important, shift in the meaning of the word 'veil' (κάλυμμα) occurs in v. 14. It is also crucial to note that Paul makes a shrewd change in the meaning of 'Moses' in v. 15. These features are worthy of some brief comment since, understandably, they offer a unique insight into Paul's use of Scripture to make his point.

In 3.7-11 the focus is on the veil of Moses himself and the meaning of the metaphor is largely contained within the bounds of the Exodus story. Yet even here there is some room for creative interpretation of Exodus 34 by Paul, though precisely what he intended to communicate by means of his reworking of the narrative is very difficult to determine. It is by no means easy to see the logical connection between Moses' concealing veil and the hardening of the hearts of the people of Israel. Generally it is assumed Paul suggests *either* that Moses hid his face because the Israelites were ashamed of their own sin and could not stand to see the glory of God reflected from his countenance, or that Moses put the veil on in order to hide from the people of Israel the fact that the glory displayed on his face was fading. Both of these interpretations have their advocates and each has a long tradition in both Judaism and Christianity. However, in vv. 12-16 the focus is on the veil as an image of the blindness of some Jews whose hearts have become hardened; their understanding is veiled and they cannot comprehend the full meaning of the old covenant. Yet the phrase 'the old covenant' in 3.14 is used only here in the Pauline letters, a fact which in itself is somewhat odd. This raises another difficult question: What does the 'old covenant' mean in this context?

It seems clear that by 'the old covenant' Paul means the covenant God made with his people at Sinai and *not* simply the Old Testament Scriptures. On this basis A.T. Hanson (1974) argues that the verb 'to pass away' (καταργεῖται) is to be associated with 'the old covenant' (τῆς παλαιᾶς διαθήκης) and not with 'the same veil' (τὸ αὐτὸ κάλυμμα). This avoids an interpretation which demands that 'the old covenant' be equated with Old Testament Scriptures. Otherwise, Hanson notes, Paul is put in the ridiculous position of suggesting that the only Scriptures he knew were abolished by the coming of Jesus Christ. Nevertheless, it should be noted here the way that Paul describes the old covenant in terms of it being embodied in Moses: 'whenever *Moses* is read a veil lies over their minds' (v. 15). This clever shift in the meaning of 'Moses' from the character in the Exodus story to the representative of the Pentateuch sets the line of argument off in a new direction and allows the quotation from Exod. 34.34 to be introduced in 3.16. Having set up the mention of 'turning to the Lord', the stage is set for Paul to clinch his argument by proclaiming the freedom that the Christian believer finds when he or she turns to the Lord Jesus Christ. This he does in dramatic fashion in vv. 17-18 (see below).

Given such provocative imagery it is hardly surprising that many interpretations of 3.7-18 assume that the inadequacy of the Mosaic law (symbolizing the old covenant) is the primary focus of attention for Paul. However, A.T. Hanson (1980) offers another interesting way of reading the passage when he suggests that the veil of Moses was used to hide the messianic glory of a pre-existent Christ from the Israelites. A positive result of this interpretation, so Hanson argues, is that the Gentiles are allowed to be enrolled in the divine plan of redemption. This shift of focus to divine glory (as opposed to an inadequate covenant) was eloquently put by C.H. Dodd some years ago:

What is it that the κάλυμμα hides? Not the true meaning of the
Old Testament but the glory of the Lord, for it is this that is seen
when the veil is removed (3.18). Christians, who have received the
Spirit and therefore enjoy liberty, see, and mirror, not the revelation of God in the Old Testament, now first properly understood,
but the glory of God in the person of Jesus Christ (2 Cor. 4.6)
(1977, p. 110).

A similar interpretation is followed in the provocative study
of R.B. Hays entitled *Echoes of Scripture in the Letters of
Paul* (1989). However, Hays argues against the related
suggestion by Hanson that it is the glory of the *pre-existent*
messiah which is in Paul's thinking within the passage. This
part of the interpretation does not necessarily need to be
adopted. As he says: 'Behind the veil is nothing other than
the glory of God, which is made visible in the face of Christ'.

The Transformation of the Believer

2 Cor. 3.18 stands as something of an enigma, particularly
since Paul here uses imagery of the believers' transformation. Given the complexities of this verse it is understandable
that Hanson (1980, p. 19) describes it as 'the sphinx among
texts'. Paul here employs an evocative verb (μεταμορφούμεθα),
used elsewhere in the undisputed Pauline letters only in
Rom. 12.2 (where it is used to refer to the 'renewal' of the
Christian mind). A number of suggestions have been put
forward to explain the reason behind the use of this image of
transformation. Some have taken it to be an indication of
Paul's reliance upon the ideas of his opponents. Others point
to the gospel stories of Jesus' transfiguration (Mt. 17.2 and
Mk 9.2), or to Jewish wisdom speculations as backgrounds.
Still others look to the widespread Graeco-Roman mythical
traditions of the day (such as Ovid's *Metamorphoses* or
Apuleius's *The Golden Ass*), some of which are known to have
parallels in Jewish Palestinian literature addressing the
divine illumination of the face or the heart. For example, J.A.
Fitzmyer (1981) discusses this at some length, calling attention to a number of Qumran texts which offer parallels,
including 1QH 4.5-6; 1QH 4.27-29; 1QS 4.28-29 and 1QS 2.2-
4. Yet another very common interpretation is to suggest that
Paul is alluding to his own conversion experience on the

Damascus road by using the image of transformation in 3.18, an allusion which is similar to what is declared in 2 Cor. 4.6.

Whatever the validity of these various suggestions, it seems clear that for Paul 3.18 is far from a digression in his thought. Rather, it forms the capstone of his argument in 3.7-18 wherein the freedom of the Christian believer is asserted—he or she has had the veil of bondage removed and is in the process of being transformed from one glory into another. In short, the temporary position of Moses has now become the permanent position of every believer in Christ. Every member of the new covenant in Christ stands in a state of openness before God; each one stands unveiled and in receipt of the eternal glory of God. Thus, it is proper to view the believers as 'those who *reflect*' (κατοπτριζόμενοι) the glory of God. However, we should note that the translation and meaning of the unusual participle κατοπτριζόμενοι is a matter of considerable debate. Some take the basic meaning to revolve around a looking glass and follow a translation along the lines of Moffatt's: 'we all *mirror* the glory of the Lord'. The point at issue is whether the basic meaning of the verb is 'to see in a mirror', or 'to reflect like a mirror'. G.B. Caird (1959, p. 391) goes so far as to suggest that 'these two renderings involve two completely different interpretations of the context and two different Christologies'. The first of these, he says, sets up a contrast between Moses, who imperfectly reflected divine glory, and Jesus, who reflected it perfectly. The second reading, on the other hand, sets up a contrast between Moses, who hides his transitory radiance with a veil, and Paul and his fellow believers, whose unveiled faces display the ever-changing glory of the Lord. It is not very hard to see how closely connected the difficult 'mirror' image in 3.18 is to the wider concerns of the Moses-New Covenant pericope of 3.1-16. Many of the same issues appear, and the interpretative debate is correspondingly related.

The description in 4.6 to 'the light of the knowledge of the glory of God in the face of Christ' has often been mentioned as a parallel to the mirror imagery contained in 3.18. This is a tempting idea, given the close association between 'glory' and 'image' contained in a number of examples from Jewish and Christian wisdom literature, including Wis. 7.25, where the figure of wisdom is described as 'a spotless mirror of the working of God, and an image of his goodness'; and *Odes* 13.1, where the author declares that 'the Lord is our mirror' (B. Witherington [1994] discusses this). In addition, as J. Murphy-O'Connor (1986, p. 53) points out, there is an interesting parallel to this sense of the rare verb κατοπτρίζειν in Philo's *Leg. All.* 3.101 where the Alexandrian writer has Moses say to God:

> I do not wish that you should be manifested to me by means of heaven or earth or water or air or any created thing at all, *nor would I behold your form in any other mirror than in you who are God* (μηδὲ κατοπτρισαίμην ἐν ἄλλῳ τινὶ ἰδέαν ἤ ἐν σοὶ τῷ θεῷ).

It is just possible that the Corinthian opponents were familiar with Philo's thought, perhaps through the agency of Apollos, who (according to Acts 18.24) was also an Alexandrian. Thus, so the argument runs, Paul alludes to the mirror image in 3.18 as a way of countering an over-inflated evaluation they have of Moses. Instead, Paul suggests that *all Christians* are beholding the glory of God and are being transformed as a result.

One final point needs to be made concerning the climactic declaration of 3.18. One might reasonably ask: What is the purpose of the transformation of the Christian believers, their 'being changed from one degree of glory into another'? Why does Paul seem to make so much of this provocative image? Is it not the fact that he wishes to stress the idea of reconciliation as foundational to any understanding of ministry? This applies not only to his self-understanding as one who is charged with 'the ministry of reconciliation' (2 Cor. 5.18), but also serves as the grounds for his earnest desire that his relationship with the Corinthians might be set right, that they 'be reconciled to God' (2 Cor. 5.20). If this is correct, then we may see the idea of the believers being gloriously transformed finding its fulfilment in their demonstrating the righteousness of God (2 Cor. 5.21) in their relations one with another.

Suggestions for Further Reading

On Moses and the New Covenant Motif
L.L. Belleville, *Reflections of Glory: Paul's Polemical Use of the Moses-Doxa Tradition in 2 Corinthians 3.12-18* (JSNTSup, 52; Sheffield: JSOT Press, 1991).
—'Tradition or Creation? Paul's Use of the Exodus 34 Tradition in 2 Corinthians 3.7-18', in C.A. Evans and J.A. Sanders (eds.), *Paul and the Scriptures of Israel* (JSNTSup, 83; Sheffield: JSOT Press, 1993), pp. 143-64.
G.B. Caird, 'Everything to Everyone: The Theology of the Corinthian Epistles', *Int* 13 (1959), pp. 387-99.
C.H. Dodd, 'New Testament Translation Problems II: 2 Corinthians 3.6', *BT* 28 (1977), pp. 110-12.
J.D.G. Dunn, '2 Corinthians III.17—"The Lord Is the Spirit" ', *JTS* 21 (1970), pp. 309-20.
A.T. Hanson, 'The Midrash in II Corinthians 3. A Reconsideration', *JSNT* 9 (1980), pp. 2-28.
S.B. Heiny, '2 Corinthians 2.14–4.6. The Motive for Metaphor', in K.H. Richards (ed.), *Society of Biblical Literature 1987 Seminar Papers* (Atlanta: Scholars Press, 1987), pp. 1-22.
C.J.A. Hickling, 'The Sequence of Thought in II Corinthians, Chapter Three', *NTS* 21 (1975), pp. 380-95.
P.R. Jones, 'The Apostle Paul: Second Moses to the New Covenant Community', in J.W. Montgomery (ed.), *God's Inerrant Word* (Minneapolis: Bethany Fellowship, 1974), pp. 219-41.
J.L. Lambrecht, 'Structure and Line of Thought in 2 Corinthians 2,14–4,6', *Bib* 64 (1983), pp. 344-80.
W. Lane, 'Covenant: The Key to Paul's Conflict with Corinth', *TB* 33 (1982), pp. 3-29.
J. Murphy-O'Connor, 'Pneumatikoi and Judaizers in 2 Cor. 2.14–4.6', *ABR* 34 (1986), pp. 42-58.
—'The New Covenant in the Letters of Paul and the Essene Documents', in M.P. Horgan and P.J. Kobelski (eds.), *To Touch the Text: Biblical and Related Studies in Honor of Joseph A. Fitzmyer, S.J.* (New York: Crossroad, 1989), pp. 194-204.
C.C. Newman, *Paul's Glory-Christology: Tradition and Rhetoric* (NovTSup, 69; Leiden: Brill, 1992).
T.E. Provence, ' "Who Is Sufficient for these Things?": An Exegesis of 2 Corinthians ii 15–iii 18', *NovT* 24 (1982), pp. 54-81.
E. Richard, 'Polemics, Old Testament, and Theology: A Study of II Cor., III, 1–IV, 6', *RB* 88 (1981), pp. 340-67.
S. Schulze, ' "Die Decke des Moses": Untersuchungen zu einer vorpaulinischen Überlieferung in 2 Cor. iii 7-18', *ZNW* 49 (1958), pp. 1-30.
C.K. Stockhausen, *Moses' Veil and the Glory of the New Covenant* (AnBib, 116; Rome: Pontifical Biblical Institute, 1989).
—'2 Corinthians 3 and the Principles of Pauline Exegesis', in C.A. Evans

and J.A. Sanders (eds.), *Paul and the Scriptures of Israel* (JSNTSup, 83; Sheffield: JSOT Press, 1993), pp. 143-64.

S. Westerholm, 'Letter and Spirit: The Foundation of Pauline Ethics', *NTS* 30 (1984), pp. 229-48.

On the Transformation of the Believer (2 Cor. 3.18)

J.A. Fitzmyer, 'Glory Reflected on the Face of Christ (2 Cor. 3.7-4.6) and a Palestinian Jewish Motif', *TS* 42 (1981), pp. 630-44.

J. Lambrecht, 'Transformation in 2 Cor. 3,18', *Bib* 64 (1983), pp. 243-54.

C.F.D. Moule, '2 Cor. 3.18b, καθάπερ ἀπὸ κυρίου πνεύματος', in H. Baltensweiler and B. Reicke (eds), *Neues Testament und Geschichte: Festschrift für Oscar Cullmann* (Tübingen: J.C.B. Mohr [Paul Siebeck], 1972), pp. 231-37. [Reprinted in *Essays in New Testament Interpretation* (Cambridge: Cambridge University Press, 1982), pp. 227-34.]

W.C. Van Unnik, ' "With Unveiled Face"; An Exegesis of 2 Corinthians iii 12-18', *NovT* 6 (1963), pp. 153-69.

B. Witherington, III, *Jesus the Sage: The Pilgrimage of Wisdom* (Edinburgh: T. & T. Clark, 1994), pp. 314-19.

N.T. Wright, *The Climax of the Covenant: Christ and the Law in Pauline Theology* (Edinburgh: T. & T. Clark, 1991), pp. 175-92. [A revised version of the author's 'Reflected Glory: 2 Corinthians 3.18', in L.D. Hurst and N.T. Wright (eds.), *The Glory of Christ in the New Testament: Studies in Christology in Memory of George B. Caird* (Oxford: Clarendon Press, 1987), pp. 139-50.]

5

IDENTIFYING THE CORINTHIAN OPPONENTS: A PROBLEM IN DETECTION

THAT THE CONGREGATION at Corinth was a difficult one, prone to quarrelling and divisions, is clear from the Pauline letters to the church. That the congregation at Corinth caused Paul many sleepless nights, and pushed him to the limits of human patience and charity, also seems indicated by the extant correspondence. Not only did they challenge the very foundation of Paul's apostolic ministry among them, but they offered a serious challenge to his understanding of the nature of Christian existence as the life of a new covenant people. Little wonder then that Karl Barth (*The Epistle to the Romans*, 1933, p. 258) once described 2 Corinthians as a 'long-drawn-out, harassed groan' from the apostle as he struggled, by means of his letters, to keep the Corinthians from self-destructing and fragmenting into splinter-groups. Indeed, if the later letter of *1 Clement* (written to the Corinthians in about 96 CE) is anything to go by, it seems that this tendency to division was not eradicated by Paul's epistles to the Corinthians, for the author, traditionally described as the bishop of Rome, laments their continued divisiveness:

> Why are there strife and passion and divisions and schisms and war among you?...Your schism has turned aside many, has cast many into discouragement, many to doubt, all of us to grief; and your sedition continues. (46.5, 9; Loeb translation).

The question of who Paul's opponents were within his various letters is a matter which has long occupied scholar-

ship. The problem is all the more significant when we come
to discussing 2 Corinthians, so intertwined is it with virtu-
ally every topic addressed in the canonical letter. As E.P.
Sanders puts it (1986, p. 84): 'The identity of the opponents
in 2 Corinthians is as vexed a problem as one can find in
Pauline studies'. At the same time, the question of who Paul
is addressing in 2 Corinthians has important implications for
evaluating the interpretation we give to the letter as a whole;
we could even describe the question of the opponents of
2 Corinthians as the hermeneutical key to the epistle itself.
Most of the leading New Testament scholars have had a go
at tackling the question at some time during their careers,
with several contributions continuing to figure regularly in
discussions of the Corinthian correspondence, notably those
by G. Friedrich (1963), J.J. Gunther (1973), D. Georgi (1987)
and C.K. Barrett (1982). Nevertheless, it is fair to say that no
consensus has been reached despite all the scholarly attention which has been dedicated to it. Indeed, in view of the
diversity of opinion on the subject, and the intractable nature
of the problem, scholarly attention has recently shifted away
from the identity of the opponents themselves to the method-
ologies employed in identifying them—always a sure sign
that an impasse has been reached.

One preliminary point needs to be set forth before we
consider the question of who the opponents might be that
Paul engages in 2 Corinthians.

The Relationship of the Opponents in
2 Corinthians 10–13 to the Parties of 1 Corinthians 1.12

It is impossible to discuss the question of who Paul's opponents were within 2 Corinthians without addressing the
complex issue of the Corinthian factionalism hinted at in
1 Cor. 1.12-17. Within this passage the division of the congregation into groups associated with Peter, Paul and Apollos is
certainly treated with derision by the apostle. His interjec-
tion of a 'Christ-party' to the list of faction leaders given in
1.12 seems deliberately intended to shame the church and
cause them to see the ridiculous nature of their divisions.
The other various groups to which Paul alludes are perhaps

best seen as representing real factions within the church. It is all too easy to *assume* that Paul was facing one united group of opponents in Corinth. However, as we all know, human dynamics are much more complicated than that and rarely are things as cut and dried as we like to make out, particularly when it comes to tensions within a church. It is perhaps nearer the truth then, if it is assumed that, at various times and in varying circumstances, Paul was faced with a number of different factions within the church, each with its own agenda, and each with a particular part to play in making up the complex whole. No doubt there were many differences among the various congregational members as well, even though Paul's letters do not afford us an opportunity to do more than guess at them. In short, it is rather unlikely that Paul was facing in Corinth a united front which held a single, fixed theological position (as W. Baird 1990 rightly argues). This is certainly true for 1 Corinthians, and there is no compelling reason to think that the situation has changed substantially by the time Paul was writing (the various letters making up) 2 Corinthians.

Having said that, we do have to contend with 1 Cor. 1.12 where the various camps are specifically named. Given the prominence of Peter within the New Testament, and the fact that in Gal. 2.11-14 Paul himself speaks of a clash he had with Peter, it is not surprising that his role in the party-divisions has attracted the lion's share of scholarly attention. For example, T.W. Manson (1962) stresses the role that the so-called Petrine party had in channelling the Jewish-Christian criticisms about Paul to the congregation in Corinth. Whether Peter himself was involved in this, or whether a group within the church was simply using his name and authority to promote their own views, is impossible to determine. Yet both T.W. Manson (1962) and C.K. Barrett (1982) posit Peter's actual presence in Corinth and view this as something of a bridge between 1 Corinthians and 2 Corinthians 10–13, even though they have different opinions of the chronological relationship of the two letters.

The Identity of the False Apostles
of 2 Corinthians 10–13

Several different theories about who the false apostles that
Paul is confronting in 2 Corinthians might have been have
been put forward. Space does not allow me to give more than
a brief introduction to this complex matter and lay out some
of the most favoured possibilities for consideration. I shall
group the scholarly attempts at unravelling the mystery of
the identity of Paul's opponents under three main headings.
However, the nature of the problem is such that the divisions
between these three groups are by no means water-tight, and
there is a great deal of overlap and fluidity between them. At
times it is only subtle differences of stress that separate one
scholarly reconstruction from another, particularly when we
come to differentiate between the gnostics and the spiritual
enthusiasts (often described as pneumatics or charismatics).
Somewhat surprisingly, important figures of Christianity
have been associated with each of these three proposals as
scholars have attempted to anchor the movement around an
apostolic figure with whom Paul is in dispute. However,
perhaps this is not as unexpected as it might first seem,
given the role of an apostle in early Christianity and the
tendency to locate the apostolic ministry in selected and
properly designated individuals. The fact that Paul occasionally uses singular expressions when describing the opponents
(especially in 2 Cor. 10–13) might also indicate that they
were gathered around one particular individual.

Judaizers (including Peter and / or James?)
Many feel that the change of vocabulary in 2 Corinthians
10–13 suggests that Paul is dealing with a new situation and
that the problems surrounding wisdom and gnosis (so characteristic of 1 Cor. 1–3) are no longer being addressed in
these chapters. C.K. Barrett contends that 2 Corinthians
10–13 is directed against outsiders who have come into
the church, rather than against the native members
of the Christian congregation (he cites 2 Cor. 10.12-18; 11.4-
5, 12-15, 22-23 and 12.1ff. in support of this). Moreover,
Barrett's contention is that these outsiders were the

Jerusalem apostles and that they were promoting the same
sort of Judaizing which we see Paul tackling in Galatians
(and Philippians?). It may well be that Peter himself visited
the church at Corinth, stirring up a theological hornet's nest
about the validity of the Mosaic law for Gentiles by his mere
presence among them. If that is the case, then the obscure
references to the unnamed opponent Paul faced at Corinth
(1 Cor. 3.10-17; 2 Cor. 5.12; 10.7-11; 11.4, 19-20) have a focal
point, namely the apostle Peter himself having freshly
arrived from Jerusalem. Indeed, 2 Cor. 10.12-14 has been
seen by some as suggesting the arrival of an envoy from
Jerusalem, assuming that Paul's association with Antioch is
what lies behind the sarcastic comment that *they* (the opponents) claim to have travelled farther than *he* (Paul) did in
reaching Corinth.

In any event, it is worth noting that Barrett (1982) follows
the lead of E. Käsemann (1942) in arguing that the 'super
apostles' (ὑπερλίαν ἀπόστολοι) referred to in 2 Cor. 11.5 and
12.11 are not to be identified with the 'false apostles'
(ψευδαπόστολοι) of 11.13, although they are to be equated
with the Jerusalem apostles, the 'pillars' (στῦλοι) mentioned
in Gal. 2.9. The 'false apostles', on the other hand, were emis-
saries of the Jerusalem church who had been sent to Corinth.
This is in contrast to many other interpreters who argue that
the two groups ('super apostles' and 'false apostles') are one
and the same, but do not think that either is necessarily to
be identified with the first apostles based in Jerusalem. The
curious reference to the 'false brothers' (ψευδαδέλφοι)
in 2 Cor. 11.26 is also of relevance here. On the basis of
the parallel found in Gal. 2.4, where the false brothers are
distinguished from the Jerusalem pillars (James, Cephas
and John), Barrett takes the false brothers of 11.26 to be
Judaizing Christians, effectively identifying them with the
false apostles of 11.13 but distinguishing them from the
super apostles of 11.5 and 12.11. In making these distinc-
tions Barrett is following the influential line of interpretation
initiated by F.C. Baur in his seminal article entitled 'Die
Christuspartei in der korinthischen Gemeinde' (1831) which
identified the super apostles with the Jerusalem apostles.
Yet Barrett differs from Baur in that he does not feel that

the Jerusalem apostles can be equated with the false apostles, since it is unlikely that Paul would describe the Jerusalem apostles in such negative language as we find in 2 Corinthians, calling them 'deceitful workmen' (11.13) and 'servants of Satan' (11.15).

However, such a clear-cut distinction between the false apostles and the super apostles has been challenged by a number of other interpreters, particularly if, as Barrett suggests, Peter had made an appearance in Corinth and stirred up trouble there. After all, is there *really* a difference between the arrival of the apostle Peter from Jerusalem and the arrival of the agents (the 'false apostles' of 11.13) sent by the church there? Thus, many agree with Barrett's central thesis identifying the Corinthian opponents as Judaizers, but do not think that the super apostles can be so readily distinguished from the false apostles. Effectively this is to take all three terms—Judaizers, false apostles and superapostles—to refer to the same group of opponents. Building on this idea, M.E. Thrall (1980) argues that the identification of the super apostles with the Jerusalem apostles may, in fact, be viewed as an extension of the synoptic tradition regarding Cephas who was at the same time both the spokesman for God and for Satan. S.E. McClelland (1982) offers a slight variation on Thrall's interpretation, suggesting that 'super apostles' was a self-designation of the opponents in Corinth. One implication of approaches such as these is that the assumption that Paul was fighting on two separate fronts in his debate with opponents in Corinth (facing not only the super apostles, who were in distant Jersualem, but also their representatives, the false apostles who were in Corinth) is rendered invalid. This is especially true if the so-called 'super apostles' were not outsiders at all, but were from within the church of Corinth itself.

The work of G. Lüdemann (1989, pp. 80-97) is similar to that of C.K. Barrett (and thus to F.C. Baur!) but gives a more elaborate form to the suggestion that Paul's Corinthian opponents are similar in theological outlook to those he encountered in the churches of Galatia. That the Galatian opponents of Paul are best viewed as similar in belief and practice to the Corinthian opponents of Paul (and, indeed,

the Philippian and Colossian heretics!) stands as one of the
most common presuppositions of New Testament scholarship. Lüdemann modifies this thesis somewhat by proposing
that the Corinthian opponents held the middle ground
between Paul and the Galatian troublemakers. Interestingly,
Lüdemann also contends (*contra* D. Georgi) that the anti-
Pauline factions of 1 Corinthians and the opponents in the
various sections of 2 Corinthians were probably the same
group. He argues this primarily on the basis of his assumption that 1 Corinthians 9 and 2 Cor. 10.12-17 both have the
Jerusalem conference as their backdrop.

In any event, the lack of any reference to the crucial issue of
circumcision as a rallying cry for such a Judaizing approach
to Christian faith is difficult to explain and remains the
Achilles-heel of such an interpretation as Barrett and those
who follow him propose. It does not appear that the validity
of the Mosaic Law was in debate in 2 Corinthians 10–13, the
very section of the canonical epistle where Paul attacks his
opponents most harshly. In fact, the word 'law' (νόμος) does
not even appear within these chapters. Thus, despite the
eloquent arguments and careful manoeuvrings explaining
the lack of any reference to circumcision in 2 Corinthians,
there is little, if any, evidence to support the contention that
there was in Corinth an active group of Jewish Christians
who were trying to persuade Gentile Christians to Judaize.

However, it should not be forgotten that there seems to
have been a significant Jewish presence within the ancient
city of Corinth in Paul's day. The discovery of a partial
inscription of eight characters, found near the entrance to
the agora on the Lechaion road and first published in 1904,
points in this direction. The reconstructed text of the inscription reads 'Synagogue of the Hebrews' ([ΣΥΝ]ΑΓΩΓΗ
ΕΒΡ[ΑΙΩΝ]); the slab appears to date to the late Imperial
period. Archaeologists of the city have also discovered in the
theatre a marble impost on which three menorahs with palm
leaves are carved. Together these artifacts are generally
regarded as prime indications of a thriving Jewish community in Corinth and it is understandable that both finds
have been associated with the synagogue mentioned in
Acts 18.7-8.

Divine Men (including Stephen and the Hellenists?)
The two most important writers who attempt to identify
Paul's opponents as Hellenists actively engaged in promoting
a Divine Man (θεῖος ἀνήρ) Christology are D. Georgi (1987)
and G. Friedrich (1963). Georgi's work in particular has been
quite influential, even though it concentrates only on 2 Cor.
2.14–6.13, 7.2-4 and 10–13 (arguing that only these sections
share a common aim of addressing the danger that the
community of Corinth faces in the form of the opponents).
The assumption throughout Georgi's work is that the opponents of Paul were Hellenistic Jewish-Christian propagandists who were interested in presenting their case to the
Gentile world in an attempt to advance the cause of Christ.
In the accomplishment of their mission the opponents laid
great stress on signs and wonders, like other Jewish and
Hellenistic divine men of the time. Central to Georgi's argument in the Pauline letters is his interpretation of 2 Cor. 3.7-
18, where the figure of Moses and the Jewish law are
contrasted with the figure of Christ and the new covenant
(the propagandists took Moses to be a 'divine man' *par excel-
lence*, a view which Paul challenges strongly as heretical).
One significant feature of Georgi's case sets it apart from
many other attempts at identifying the Corinthian opponents
of Paul. He argues that the Hellenistic-Jewish apologists
arrived in Corinth only after the church there had received
Paul's second letter (our 1 Corinthians) to them. In effect,
this means that, for Georgi, the opponents Paul faces in
2 Corinthians are *not* the same ones he faced in 1 Corinthians and the allusions to the opponents given in 2 Cor. 3.1
and 11.4 are cited as evidence of this (in fact, Georgi takes
Paul to be fighting Gnostics in 1 Corinthians).

   G. Friedrich builds upon the proposals made by D. Georgi,
but the main novelty of his interpretation is that it attempts
to forge an all-important link to Stephen and the Hellenists
of Acts 6–7 in reconstructing the historical situation. A great
many similarities between the teaching and practice of the
Hellenists (of Acts) and the Hebrews (of 2 Corinthians) are
suggested by Friedrich, including a fanciful argument which
equates those designated as 'the Hellenists' (in Acts 6.1) with
those designated as 'the Hebrews' (in 2 Cor. 11.22).

D. Georgi's suggestion about the opponents of Paul being divine men (θεῖοι ἄνδρες) has been enormously influential in studies of 2 Corinthians and remains a standard work which must be reckoned with. However, the greatest weakness of this way of identifying the Corinthian opponents of Paul with Hellenistic-Jewish propagandists motivated by a Divine-Man theology is the lack of evidence for the widespread influence of a θεῖος ἀνήρ Christology during the first century CE. If the idea of a θεῖος ἀνήρ cannot be substantiated (and many do not believe that it can be), the theory collapses like a house of cards.

Gnostics and Spiritual Enthusiasts (including Apollos?)
That Paul was combatting a full-blown Gnosticism in Corinth has often been argued, particularly by German scholarship of the earlier part of this century, following the lead of W. Lütgert who first argued the case in 1908. R. Bultmann (1985) has been an important advocate of the Gnostic solution to the identity of the Corinthian opponents, but it is the name of W. Schmithals (1971) that is most often associated with it.

The suggestion that at least some members of the congregation felt that their emphasis on wisdom was confirmed by the demonstration of charismatic and spiritual gifts does make sense of many parts of 1 Corinthians, notably the *pneumatikos/psuchikos* contrast underlying such passages as 1.18–3.20, 12-14 and 15.46-47. But can this be used as a basis for identifying Paul's opponents in 2 Corinthians (assuming of course that he is facing the same group of opponents here as he was in 1 Corinthians)? Probably not, given the severe methodological problems in using Gnostic texts as a means of unlocking the secrets of the New Testament documents. At the very least, descriptions of the Corinthian opponents as 'Gnostics' need to be avoided, as if they were card-carrying members of a formal philosophical party. Many commentators prefer to describe the opponents as '*proto-gnostics*', and the loosely-organized philosophical movement to which they belonged as 'incipient gnosticism'.

With this proviso, the essential point of a controversy about wisdom being the heart of the controversy in Corinth

may still yield results, particularly when it is tied to a careful discussion about the role of Apollos in the church at
Corinth. The frequent reference to Apollos in 1 Corinthians,
specifically in connection with what appears to have been a
developing personality cult, is significant and overlaps somewhat with the arguments surrounding gnostic influences in
Corinth (Apollos is mentioned in 3.4-6, 22; 4.6). Indeed,
Barrett (1982, p. 4) goes so far as to suggest that 'Apollos
contributed to the Corinthian development of thought about
γνῶσις, λόγος and σοφία.' In other words, the suggestion is
that Apollos was the popularizer of a brand of preaching
which concentrated on wisdom and he (inadvertently) made
that the focal point of his understanding of Christian faith,
effectively playing into the hands of a faction of the
Corinthian church. Indeed, the suggestion that Apollos,
while he was staying in Ephesus between the years 52–54
CE, wrote what we now call the epistle to the Hebrews to the
church at Corinth has occasionally been put forward. This
builds on an assumption about 1 Cor. 16.12 as hinting at
Apollos's reluctance to promote the factionalism which has
become associated with his name, and an equation of the
'Hebrews' of 2 Cor. 11.22 with the congregation at large.
There is much to be said for this as a proposal, although we
would need to be careful not to allow such a suggestion to
become entangled with the idea that Apollos and his
followers were Gnostics in the technical sense of the term To
take this step of interpretation is to fall headlong into the
trap of anachronism. F. Watson (1986) is the most recent,
and most able, advocate of the suggestion that the false apostles of 2 Corinthians 10–13 are, in fact, Apollos and his
companions. As Watson summarizes:

> [T]he false apostles show remarkable resemblances to Apollos.
> Like Apollos, they come to Corinth armed with a letter of recom-
> mendation from another church. Like Apollos, they were Jewish
> Christians who do not seem to have been interested in imposing
> the law on Gentiles. Like Apollos, they were more eloquent
> speakers than Paul. They visited Corinth at exactly the time when
> a visit from Apollos might have been expected (p. 84).

However, not many would agree that Apollos had such a
prominent role as an instigator among Paul's opponents as

Watson suggests. Watson's opinion stands in stark contrast
to the opinion of F.F. Bruce (1977) who comments:

> In his references to Apollos Paul shows no trace of reserve; every
> mention he makes of him is marked by friendliness and
> confidence. Apollos's teaching evidently commanded Paul's
> approval (p. 257).

Nevertheless, a number of scholars have looked to the
mysterious Apollos to help solve the question of the identity
of Paul's opponents in Corinth and he seems destined to
figure in any discussion. Moreover, the stress laid upon
knowledge and wisdom as central themes in the beliefs of the
opponents, together with the evident high regard with which
charismatic gifts were held in Corinth, is almost certainly
correct.

These features of church life in Corinth have led many
others, perhaps even the majority of scholars writing in the
last dozen years or so, to suggest that the opponents were
spiritual enthusiasts or pneumatics, probably Hellenistic-
Jewish Christians with some connections with Jerusalem but
not official representatives of the church there. In short, the
origins of the opponents in Corinth lie in Diaspora Judaism,
not the Jerusalem mother church. Even the unlikely proposal
by J. Murphy-O'Connor (1986), that the opponents in Corinth
consisted of two groups (pneumatics *and* Judaizers) who had
forged an alliance against Paul, accepts the validity of this
point, at least as far as the pneumatics are concerned.
Although it must be recognized that it is difficult to define
precisely what is meant by the terms 'spiritual enthusiasts'
and 'pneumatics', most who follow this approach assume that
the overemphasis on spiritual matters has at its heart a challenge to Paul's apostleship. His opponents rejected Paul's
authority on the grounds that he was not spiritual enough
and that his ministry did not provide what they thought to
be the evidence of a charismatic apostleship. This, for
example, is the conclusion of the most recent study of the
subject, that by J.L. Sumney (1993) which attempts to adopt
an objective historical methodology in tackling the issue. In
some ways the discussion has come full circle insofar as
Sumney echoes many of the conclusions of E. Käsemann
whose seminal article on the subject was published over half

a century ago in 1942. In contentious matters such as establishing the identity of Paul's opponents 'what goes around
comes around'.

Suggestions for Further Reading

On the Corinthian Opponents
P.W. Barnett, 'Opposition in Corinth', *JSNT* 22 (1984), pp. 3-17.
E.E. Ellis, *Prophecy and Hermeneutic in Early Christianity* (Grand Rapids:
    Eerdmans, 1978), pp. 80-115 and 116-28.
G. Friedrich, 'Die Gegner des Paulus im 2. Korintherbrief', in O. Betz,
    M. Hengel and W.G. Kümmel (eds.), *Abraham unser Vater: Festschrift
    für Otto Michel* (Leiden: Brill, 1963), pp. 1-12.
D. Georgi, *The Opponents of Paul in Second Corinthians* (ET; Edinburgh:
    T. & T. Clark, 1987 [1964]).
J.J. Gunther, *St. Paul's Opponents and their Background: A Study of
    Apocalyptic and Jewish Sectarian Writings* (NovTSup, 35; Leiden: Brill,
    1973).
R.P. Martin, 'The Opponents of Paul in 2 Corinthians: An Old Issue
    Revisited', in G.F. Hawthorne and O. Betz (eds.), *Tradition and
    Interpretation in the New Testament: Essays in Honor of E. Earle Ellis*
    (Grand Rapids: Eerdmans, 1987), pp. 279-87.
S.E. McClelland, ' "Super-Apostles, Servants of Christ, Servants of Satan": A
    Response', *JSNT* 14 (1982), pp. 82-87.
J. Murphy-O'Connor, 'Pneumatikoi and Judaizers in 2 Cor. 2.14-4.6', ABR
    34 (1986), pp. 42-58.
P. Richardson, 'The Thunderbolt in Q and the Wise Man in Corinth', in
    P. Richardson and J.C. Hurd (eds.), *From Jesus to Paul: Studies in
    Honour of Francis Wright Beare* (Waterloo, Ontario: Wilfrid Laurier
    University Press, 1984), pp. 91-111.
E.P. Sanders, 'Paul on the Law, his Opponents, and the Jewish People in
    Philippians 3 and 2 Corinthians 11', in P. Richardson and D. Granskou
    (eds.), *Anti-Judaism in Early Christianity. I. Paul and the Gospels*
    (SCJ, 2; Waterloo, Ontario: Wilfrid Laurier University Press, 1986),
    pp. 75-90.
J.P. Sampley, 'Paul, his Opponents in 2 Corinthians 10–13, and the
    Rhetorical Handbooks', in J. Neusner, P. Borgen, E.S. Frerichs and
    R. Horsley (eds.), *The Social World of Formative Christianity and
    Judaism: In Tribute to Howard Clark Kee* (Philadelphia: Fortress Press,
    1988), pp. 162-77.
M.E. Thrall, 'Super-Apostles, Servants of Christ, and Servants of Satan',
    JSNT 6 (1980), pp. 42-57.

6

PAUL AND THE
JERUSALEM COLLECTION

AN INVESTIGATION of Paul's role in the gathering of the Jerusalem collection is essential for any serious study of 2 Corinthians. The matter was clearly one about which the apostle was concerned in his correspondence to the church in Corinth and it looms large in the background of both 1 and 2 Corinthians. Indeed, 2 Corinthians 8–9 are generally regarded as being given over specifically to a discussion of the matter and may even have been written as separate letters dealing with the administration of the collection. Yet somewhat ironically, despite the central position the collection holds in Paul's strategy of promoting inter-church relationships, neither the delivery of the collection nor the method of its administration are matters which are explicitly discussed anywhere in the Pauline letters. In any event, as an indication of its centrality D. Georgi (1992, pp. 196-97) lists 25 different words and phrases in passages in Paul's letters which deal with the collection. Older suggestions that the collection was in fact some sort of Temple tax (like that mentioned in Mt. 17.24-27) imposed by the church leadership in Jerusalem upon the Gentile believers, who were their spiritual heirs (cf. Rom. 15.27), are generally regarded as untenable nowadays. However, the half-shekel Temple tax may be responsible for the idea of collecting funds throughout the diaspora and channelling them back to the home base in Jerusalem. In this respect, at least, it could be seen as an analogy, although it should not be taken to be an exact parallel to the Jerusalem fund.

In 1 Cor. 16.1-4 Paul writes to the church at Corinth of his
intentions concerning the collection, probably sending the
letter via his colleague Titus. Here he exhorts the
Corinthians to begin a systematic programme of gathering
together money for the Jerusalem collection, as had the
churches in Galatia. In addition, Paul tells them of his plans
to visit Corinth in the near future so that he may facilitate
transfer of the collection to Jerusalem. However, following
the sending of 1 Corinthians it appears that Paul changes
his mind about the arrangements (why is not entirely clear),
and instead he sends Titus and another unnamed colleague
to re-launch the gathering of the collection. Several passages
in the canonical 2 Corinthians allude to this, including 8.6,
10; 9.2 and 12.18. Paul is forcefully reminding the Corinthians of their prior commitment to financial assistance of
the church in Jerusalem and holds them to their pledge,
probably made a year or so earlier (2 Cor. 8.10-15; cf. 9.2).
We can assume that the church at Corinth included some
wealthy members and that it had sufficient resources to
make a substantial contribution to the effort.

It appears that a major part of the so-called Third
Missionary Journey (as described in Acts 18.23–21.26) was
given over to the promotion of the collection project. Perhaps
this collection was a follow-up to the relief fund which the
church of Antioch sent to the church at Jerusalem via Paul
and Barnabas, an incident which is recorded in Acts 11.27-
30. Indeed, K.F. Nickle (1966, p. 26) describes this event as
'the prototype for Paul's great collection among his Gentile
churches for the Jerusalem church'. The delivery of the
collection in Jerusalem is alluded to at several points within
the narrative of Acts (20.16, 22; 24.17), although the motif
does not appear to have a prominent place within the narrative of the book itself. Yet it must be acknowledged that the
whole issue is complicated somewhat by the considerable
debate about how many times Paul actually visited
Jerusalem (was it three, or four, or five?).

So how successful was Paul in his arrangements regarding
the collection? There are one or two hints in 2 Corinthians
occurring in the midst of Paul's exhortations to the

Corinthians which give an indication on this matter. It
appears that the Macedonians responded generously (2 Cor.
8.3-5) and that the Philippians gave more than they could
afford (2 Cor. 8.6-11). Both examples are used by Paul to
challenge the Corinthians to consider afresh their own com-
mitments and make good their earlier promise. The apparent
year-long delay in gathering the collection is sometimes
linked to the curious allusion Paul makes in 2 Cor. 1.8
to the 'trouble in Asia'. Occasionally it has been suggested,
on the basis of this verse, that Paul was not able to organize
a collection in Asia because he had fallen out with the church
at Ephesus. However, there is no real evidence for Paul's
estrangement from the congregation in Ephesus. In fact,
there is every indication that his relationship with them was
on good terms until the end of his life.

There are three related issues which demand our attention
as we consider the matter of the collection in 2 Corinthians.

Theological Motivations for Organizing a Collection
for the Saints in Jerusalem

Precisely why it was that Paul took it upon himself to organize and promote the collection for the sake of the poor in
Jerusalem is a matter about which there is considerable
speculation. Several different theological reasons have been
suggested as motivating Paul's emphasis on the collection.

It appears from 2 Cor. 8.4 and Rom. 15.26 that Paul
viewed the collection as an act of charity wherein the well-to-
do assisted the less fortunate. There was in Judaism a long
tradition associating righteousness before God with alms-
giving and this may help explain why the collection fund was
so important for Paul. No doubt the words and actions of
Jesus himself are also significant, since he too exhorted his
followers to share their possessions with others (Mt. 6.2) and
thereby demonstrate their faithfulness. In other words, it
may be that in Paul's view the collection was a tangible
expression of Christian discipleship and those who
contributed to it were thought to be following the example of
the Lord. Thus, Paul reminds the Corinthians of the poverty
of the Lord (2 Cor. 8.9) in the hope that they too will be

generous in their contribution to the project.

Other factors may also figure in any assessment of the theological significance that Paul attached to the collection, notably that it stood as a tangible demonstration of the unity of the church worldwide and thus could be viewed as an extension of the compromise agreed at the Jerusalem Council aimed at defusing tension between Jewish Christians and Hellenistic Christians. Thus in Gal. 2.9-11 we read of Paul's commitment to 'remember the poor in Jerusalem'. However, this is a controversial passage and not all interpreters take it as referring to the collection project. For example, D. Georgi offers an important alternative reconstruction in which Paul is thought to have undertaken two separate collections, the first at the instigation of the 'pillars' of the Jerusalem Church and the second on his own initiative. Such an assessment is based largely on the fact that Paul nowhere refers to the Jerusalem conference when discussing the collection. Thus, Georgi argues against the common interpretation that the call for the Christians to 'remember the poor' in Gal. 2.10 necessarily be taken as a direct reference to the Jerusalem collection. According to him the action implied by this verb may include a financial consideration, but need not be equated exclusively with the gathering of money for the church in Jerusalem.

The Apostle's understanding of the role of the Gentiles in bringing about the eschatological redemption of the Jewish nation may also be relevant here. Thus the collection may have served as a prime demonstration of the role that the Gentile nations play in bringing about the ultimate salvation of the nation Israel. Certainly in 2 Cor. 9.13-15 Paul associates the collection with the outpouring of God's grace among the Gentiles. In short, the suggestion is that the conversion of the Gentiles (as evidenced by their financial gifts) was understood by Paul to herald the eventual conversion of the nation Israel. In effect it was part of Paul's mission strategy, which may help explain why he discusses the delivery of the collection to Jerusalem within the context of his larger apostolic mission to Spain as in Rom. 15.24-26. The collection, and the conversion of the Gentiles which it represented, was taken to be indicative of the Church as living in the last days, the time of eschatological fulfilment wherein the Gentile nations would flock to Jerusalem to worship the one true God and motivate the Jewish nation through jealousy to respond accordingly. The argument in Romans 9–11 is of paramount importance here, particularly as it juxtaposes Jewish and Gentile responses to the claims of Jesus Christ. The cryptic statement in 2 Cor. 8.13-14 is also worth noting in this regard, although not all accept that Paul saw the role of the Gentiles in either passage as a catalyst for the conversion of the Jewish nation.

While there may be something in the suggestion that Paul's eschatological beliefs contributed to his enthusiasm for the collection, it is clear that such a financial gift was seen by the apostle as a means of unifying Christian believers, both Jewish and Gentile, and as a means of effecting peace between them in the midst of a tense theological situation. As W.D. Davies puts it:

> the purpose of the collection is at least to recognize equality between Gentile and Jerusalem Christians, the establishment of a true ecumenicity (1994, p. 201).

In any event, Rom. 15.30-31 seems to indicate, somewhat ironically, that Paul was not altogether welcome in Jerusalem even though he was bearing a financial gift for the church there. In these verses Paul goes so far as to describe his antagonists in Judaea as 'unbelievers' (τῶν ἀπειθούντων). Some have even suggested that the Jerusalem church refused to accept the collection, lest acceptance of it be viewed as tacit agreement with Paul's theological position on the thorny question of Jewish/Gentile relations. Paul may have been viewed by the powers-that-be in Jerusalem as an apostate, and acceptance of anything he had to offer was made difficult as a result. Once this possibility of an atmosphere of hostility is conceded, it is not difficult to accept the judgment of N.H. Taylor:

> The outcome of this project is unknown and would in any event be rendered irrelevant by the outbreak of the Jewish War ten years later. What is certain is that the delivery of the collection resulted, directly or indirectly, in Paul's arrest in Jerusalem and the effective termination of his missionary career (1992, p. 207).

Finally, we may see Paul's theological understanding of
reconciliation as another underlying motivation for the
collection. In 5.18-19 Paul emphasizes how important the
theme of reconciliation is, describing it as a 'ministry'
(διακονία) with which both he and the Corinthians have been
entrusted (it may be significant that the term διακονία is
elsewhere used of the collection itself). Paul may have felt
that by making a financial contribution to the collection
effort the Corinthians were demonstrating the outworking of
this ministry of reconciliation in their lives. Of course, it goes
without saying that by exhorting the church to put this God-
given ministry into practice Paul is, at the same time,
encouraging a healing of the rift that had developed between
himself and the Corinthians. He recognized that reconciliation is a two-way street and knew that there is no better way
of overcoming estrangement between two parties than by
uniting them in a common effort.

The Deputation of Titus

In 2 Cor. 8.16-17 Paul declares to the Corinthians that he is
sending Titus to them on a return visit. Titus, who Paul
stresses had a genuine affection for and abiding interest in
the congregation at Corinth (witness 2 Cor. 7.6-7, 13-15), is
sent to serve as the apostolic agent with respect to the collection. That such envoys as Timothy and Titus were important
figures within the Pauline churches, particularly when it
came to the collection for the saints in Jerusalem, is clear.
Prevailing attitudes and expectations in the first-century
Hellenistic world about the role and function of ambassadors
and diplomatic envoys offer an important backdrop for the
New Testament in this respect and have been an important
area of recent research. For example, they provide us with an
opportunity against which to assess key passages within the
Pauline letters, such as Paul's description of himself as one
serving as an ambassador of Christ (2 Cor. 5.20). In the light
of this background we may also better understand Paul's
delegation of authority to Titus, sending him as he does to
the Corinthians to serve as apostolic representative. This is
probably not the first time that Titus served as Paul's envoy
to the church at Corinth. If, as was suggested earlier, Paul

wrote the so-called 'severe letter' to the Corinthians in the summer of 55 while staying in Ephesus, it is most likely that Titus was the one who delivered it (this would have been his first encounter with the Corinthian congregation). The fact that in 2 Corinthians 8 Titus is once again delegated with wide powers also indicates something about the place and authority of such appointed envoys. This is especially so given the fact that Titus is not only charged with responsibility for patching up the strained relationship between the church and Paul (following the apostle's disastrous visit of 2 Cor. 2.1; 12.21; 13.2), but also with making the arrangements for the relaunch of the Jerusalem collection itself (2 Cor. 7.6-7, 13-15). The fact that Paul could even consider raising the matter of the collection again with the Corinthians is testimony to the success of the work of Titus among them.

Nevertheless, given such a positive portrait that Paul seems to paint of his colleague and fellow-labourer Titus, it is somewhat surprising that he is never mentioned within the narrative of Acts. Perhaps this is due to a reluctance on the part of the author to include reference to someone as controversial as Titus obviously was, a figure deeply embroiled in many of the disputes of the first-century church, notably the debate over circumcision.

R.P. Martin (1986, p. 249), as part of his argument for the independence of 2 Corinthians 8, argues that the chapter was written just after Titus had arrived in Macedonia from Corinth and was reunited with Paul. He suggests Titus was about to leave again for Corinth carrying with him Paul's letter to the church there (which has survived in the form of 2 Cor. 1.1–2.13; 7.5-16), with an additional chapter (2 Cor. 8) being sent to Corinth via the agency of the brethren designated to accompany Titus (mentioned in 2 Cor. 8.17-18). As an addendum to this interpretation, it is to be noted that ch. 9 is taken to have been written subsequently to this extra ch. 8 and appears to be addressed to a wider audience, namely the province of Achaia (as seems indicated by 9.2).

Finally, we note that the deputation of Titus is also alluded to briefly in 2 Cor. 12.16-18 where Paul addresses veiled accusations about his own conduct in the gathering of the collection (see below).

The Identity of the Two Guardians

Paul mentions the appointment of two other guardians to
supervise the collection on no less than three occasions
(2 Cor. 8.18-19; 22-23; 9.5). Who these two figures are has
remained a mystery, as has the geographical base of their
church involvement. When Paul says that they are appointed
by 'the churches' (8.18, 19, 23, 24) what does he have in
mind? Does he mean the Jerusalem church or, as is
commonly held, the Macedonian churches, notably the
congregations at Philippi and Thessalonica? It is impossible
to decide with any degree of certainty, although K.F. Nickle
(1966, pp. 19-22) argues strongly against the identification of
the Macedonian churches as the appointing body (instead he
proposes that the two figures concerned were Judas [2 Cor.
8.18-19[and Silas [2 Cor. 8.22] and that they were associated
with the church at Jerusalem). On the strength of Acts 20.4
Sopater of Beroea or Aristarchus and Secundus of Thessalonica have been suggested as possible candidates. The precise purpose in having two guardians accompany the delivery
of the collection to Jerusalem is never made entirely clear.
One suggestion is that they were appointed to represent their
communities (local Jewish communities in the Diaspora) at
the sacrifices offered in Jerusalem. A much more likely
reason is that they were introduced as guarantors of the safe
transport of the collection funds to Jerusalem. Perhaps Paul
even insisted upon them to safeguard himself against any
possible charges of embezzlement. In any event the high
praise accorded to the unnamed pair by the apostle suggests
that they were well-known and trusted figures of the early
Church.

Accusations about Financial Impropriety

That Paul had to act prudently with regard to the collection
and avoid opening himself to any suggestions of financial
misconduct seems indicated by 2 Cor. 8.20-21. The verses are
a model of tact: 'We intend that no one should blame us
about this liberal gift which we are administering, for we aim
at what is honorable not only in the Lord's sight but also in

the sight of men.' Paul here cites the second half of a couplet from Prov 3.3-4, which contains many key ideas central to his message to the Corinthians. Not only are loyalty and faithfulness mentioned in 3.3, but so too is the image of having such qualities 'engraved upon the tablet of one's heart' (an image used earlier by Paul to great effect in the midst of his discussion of Moses and the New Covenant in 2 Cor. 3–4.6). It is not difficult to imagine that the collection became a proving ground for Paul's authority as an apostle within the church at Corinth.

Similarly, 2 Cor. 12.16 is sometimes interpreted as an indication that there was an additional accusation that Paul swindled the collection money out of the Corinthians and used it for his own purposes. On the basis of the passage M.M. Mitchell (1994, p. 8) wryly remarks that the Corinthians may have thought Paul 'guilty of double deceit and mail fraud in his attempt to fleece the Corinthians from a distance'. The verse itself is rather enigmatic: 'But granting that I myself did not burden you, I was crafty, you say, and got the better of you by guile'. Perhaps such questions about financial impropriety with regard to the collection help explain why Paul is said elsewhere to travel to Jerusalem surrounded by a large number of Gentile Christians (Acts 20.4). Doubts among the Corinthians about Paul's financial trustworthiness may also explain the lengths to which Paul goes in arranging stewards, including the faithful Titus, to accompany the collection to Jerusalem (2 Cor. 8.16-24). He is anxious to act with propriety and publicly to be seen to do so. As F.W. Danker (1989, p. 169) puts it: Paul wants to make it clear that he 'did not take the Corinthians to the cleaners. He was no sponger.'

One concluding remark dealing with chronological matters is worth mentioning in connection with the collection. The fact that 2 Cor. 12.16-18 appears to look back upon the visit of Paul's deputation, while 2 Corinthians 8–9 view it as a future prospect is generally taken as lending support to the suggestion that 2 Corinthians 10–13 was written *after* 2 Corinthians 1–9 (and thus was not part of the 'severe letter').

Suggestions for Further Reading

On the Jerusalem Collection

C.R. Buck, 'The Collection for the Saints', *HTR* 43 (1950), pp. 1-29.

W.D. Davies, *The Gospel and the Land: Early Christianity and Jewish Territorial Doctrine* (Biblical Seminar, 25; Sheffield: JSOT Press, 1994), pp. 200-19.

L.W. Hurtado, 'The Jerusalem Collection and the Book of Galatians', *JSNT* 5 (1979), pp. 46-62.

J. Knox, 'Chapters in a Life of Paul—A Response to Robert Jewett and Gerd Luedemann', in B. Corley (ed.), *Colloquy on New Testament Studies: A Time for Reappraisal and Fresh Approaches* (Macon, GA: Mercer University Press, 1983), pp. 339-64.

S. McKnight, 'Collection for the Saints', in G.F. Hawthorne, R.P. Martin and D.G. Reid (eds.), *Dictionary of Paul and his Letters* (Leicester: Inter-Varsity Press, 1993), pp. 143-47.

M.M. Mitchell, 'Rhetorical Shorthand in Pauline Argumentation: The Functions of "The Gospel" in the Corinthian Correspondence', in L.A. Jervis and P. Richardson (eds.), *Gospel in Paul: Studies on Corinthians, Galatians and Romans for Richard N. Longenecker* (JSNTSup, 108; Sheffield: JSOT Press, 1994), pp. 63-88.

J. Munck, *Paul and the Salvation of Mankind* (London: SCM Press, 1959). pp. 282-308.

K.F. Nickle, *The Collection: A Study in Paul's Strategy* (SBT, 48; London: SCM Press, 1966).

On the Deputation of Titus

M.M. Mitchell, 'New Testament Envoys in the Context of Greco-Roman Diplomatic and Epistolary Conventions: The Example of Timothy and Titus', *JBL* 111 (1992), pp. 641-62.

W.O. Walker, 'The Timothy-Titus Problem Reconsidered', *ExpTim* 92 (1980–81), pp. 231-35.

7

SOME PUZZLING PASSAGES

FOR ITS SIZE 2 CORINTHIANS presents us with a unusually large number of passages which have perplexed scholars over the years. Some of these passages contain particular grammatical or exegetical problems which require special attention; others allude to historical events about which we have little (or no!) extra information to help anchor them within a chronological framework; still others contain difficulties of theological interpretation. Within this chapter I have selected ten of these perplexing passages, introduced by key phrases contained within them, and will offer some extended discussion of the passages as a whole. The aim is not to be comprehensive within the discussion; space does not allow us to do more than highlight some of the more significant interpretative suggestions. Rather the intention here is to use these passages as windows through which to gain a better of the view of the terrain which is 2 Corinthians. These puzzling passages provide an opportunity to see the type and range of scholarly techniques which have been applied to the interpretation of the epistle, especially in recent years. By examining them in detail we can readily see that 2 Corinthians continues to be one of the most important documents in the New Testament canon, standing on the cutting edge of current critical research.

'The Affliction in Asia' (1.8-10)

This section of 2 Corinthians has been an important focus of attention in studies of the epistolary form of the document as a whole. Many feel that it is not a part of the introductory thanksgiving (1.3-7) but that it serves as the opening statement for the body of the letter which runs at least through 7.16. That Paul uses a travelogue to mark this transition is not especially unusual in itself, but what makes this paragraph difficult to interpret is the imprecision about the incident to which Paul makes allusion in v. 8. What is the 'affliction which took place in Asia', a trauma so great that it threatened the lives of Paul and his companions? One common interpretation is that the affliction refers to a life-threatening illness, perhaps the same one alluded to in 2 Cor. 12.7, Paul's 'thorn in the flesh'.

A multitude of other questions can be posed when considering the cryptic verse in 2 Cor. 1.8. Should we follow the lead of Tertullian and equate it with the curious reference in 1 Cor. 15.30-32 to Paul facing the wild beasts in Ephesus? Could it be related to Acts 19.23-41, the episode with Demetrius the silversmith over the image of Artemis, or even the incident alluded to in 2 Tim 4.16? Or is it possibly a veiled reference to the anxious time Paul spent in Troas waiting to meet with Titus and hear about the situation in Corinth? Does the lack of precision in describing the incident indicate that the Corinthians were already well aware of the details? Or is Paul's brief mention of it merely to introduce the idea as a prelude for what he anticipates he is going to have to face in his dealings with the Corinthians, effectively making out the opponents he has there as the next danger to be faced, just as he had faced Jewish opposition in Asia, and indeed in Jerusalem (as hinted at in Acts 21.27 where Jews from Asia stir up trouble for Paul)? R. Yates (1983) follows this last interpretation and identifies the antagonists Paul alludes to in 2 Cor. 1.8 as Jewish leaders in Corinth who were jealous of his success in the province of Asia. Similarly, G. Lüdemann (1984, p. 86) brings together 2 Cor. 1.8 and the statement in 1 Cor. 15.32 that Paul fought with wild beasts in order to suggest that Paul had lost his support in the city of Ephesus, and as a result the Ephesians failed to participate in the collection. However, this is rather speculative and there is no clear evidence suggesting any alienation between Paul and the members of the church in Ephesus. However,

Lüdemann is correct in pointing out the tension implied by the passages, even if he is wrong about the source of the threat, since it appears more likely that it lies with Demetrius and his commercial guild rather than with the church. It seems best that 1 Cor. 15.32 not be taken literally. Paul did not *really* fight with wild beasts in the theatre of Ephesus; the fact that he does not list such an incident in his catalogue of trials (2 Cor. 11.23-28) is a glaring omission if it were literally true. Rather, 1 Cor. 15.32 stands as a metaphorical statement about the opponents whom Paul faced in Ephesus, probably over the incident with Demetrius. If this is correct, it is but one small step to associate the 'affliction in Asia' with Paul's subsequent imprisonment in Ephesus at the hands of these opponents. Such a suggestion is strengthened by the possibility that Paul wrote to the church at Philippi during this Ephesian imprisonment, and it does provide a plausible explanation for what is, by any standard, an extremely enigmatic phrase in 2 Cor. 1.8. Thus, there is some justification in interpreting the reference in 2 Cor. 1.9 to the 'sentence of death' (ἀπόκριμα τοῦ θανάτου) in light of Phil. 1.20-23 and 2.12-18. Regardless of whether or not Paul was literally under a 'sentence of death', the seriousness of his experience in Asia should not be underestimated.

'Led Forth in Triumph' (2.14)

The precise meaning of the verb θριαμβεύειν has long been a matter of scholarly interest, and most commentators accept that the idea of a Roman military triumph is probably at its core. Nevertheless, something of the ambiguity implied by the verb is reflected in the various translations of 2 Cor. 2.14 and the way in which they communicate the force of this military image. Many translations take the central image to be a positive one wherein the believer either triumphs in Christ, or is said to triumph through Christ, or joins in the divine triumphal procession as one of the victors. A few modern translations reverse this triumphalistic note, however, and focus on the idea of the believer as one who is led as a captive in God's triumphal procession. Thus the NEB

renders the phrase: 'But thanks be to God, who continually
leads us about, captives in Christ's triumphal procession'. In
short, the question is: Does the triumph image focus on the
participants in the celebration as *victorious conquerors* or on
them as *vanquished enemies*? F.W. Farrar (1919) may well
have been right when he said (p. 410): 'St. Paul was so
possessed by the metaphor that he did not pause to disen-
tangle it'. Nevertheless, many interpreters of 2 Corinthians
have applied themselves to the arduous task of disentangle-
ment and we will endeavour to follow the main directions of
their deliberations.

Much of the recent scholarly debate about 2 Cor. 2.14 has
revolved around the proper use of lexical evidence in
interpretation. The fact that the verb θριαμβεύειν is quite
rare in Hellenistic Greek, appearing elsewhere in the New
Testament only in Col 2.15, makes it a prime target for such
speculation.

Many recent interpretations of the enigmatic verse have
been put forward, most of which are forced to employ some
specialized approach, or adopt a more comprehensive
analysis of Paul's argument in 2 Corinthians, or beyond, in
order to offer an explanation for what is in effect a puzzling
linguistic metaphor. Yet what is striking about a number of
these interpretations is the way in which they each try to
relate the imagery of the verse (whatever it might be!) to
the question of Paul's apostolic ministry. For example,
L. Williamson (1968) turns to the variety of instances in
Paul's letters in which paradoxical statements are made in
order to support the contention that the image intended by
the use of 'to triumph' (θριαμβεύειν) is that of the believer as
a conquered slave who is part of Christ's victory triumph,
and yet at the same time, a joyful participant in the Lord's
celebration parade. In effect, Paul's life as an apostle is an
expression of precisely this paradox of defeat/victory and
weakness/power. Williamson's ideas have been quite
influential and are often cited as a definitive interpretation of
2 Cor. 2.14, although he has not been without his critics. For
example, R.B. Egan (1977) questions the very foundation of
the interpretation, namely that the verb θριαμβεύειν was
understood as an image intimately linked to the Roman mili-

tary triumph. Instead Egan argues that the verb is best
translated as 'to reveal', or 'to make manifest', or to 'publi-
cize', and that this was how it was understood by most early
Christian commentators and translators. He suggests that a
better translation of the verse is: 'But thanks be to God who
is always making us known in Christ and revealing through
us the odor of his knowledge in every place'. It is to be noted
that while this interpretation dissolves any alleged connection with the military triumph imagery, it nevertheless does
still maintain a strong link to the theme at hand, effectively
constituting an introduction to Paul's apologia for his apostleship (contained in 2.14–7.4).

However, not all have been so willing to surrender the
military imagery underlying θριαμβεύειν in 2.14, although
the need to relate the metaphor to the larger concern of
Paul's apostleship is something about which there is general
agreement. Thus, S. Hafemann (1990, pp. 16-83) associates
both the triumph imagery (focusing on the word θριαμβεύειν)
and the fragrance imagery (focusing on the words 'fragrance'
[ὀσμή] and 'aroma' [εὐωδία]) with the larger issue of Paul's
apostolic authority which is being addressed in 2 Cor.
2.14–6.4. Inherent in the triumph image, Hafemann insists,
is the idea of the captives who are in the procession being led
to their deaths by their conquerors. This leads him to take
the military image as one in which Paul sees himself as a
slave who has been conquered and who is being led in the
triumphal procession by the conqueror (Jesus Christ himself)
with the apostle's life being offered to God as sacrificial
incense. In effect, Paul's view of his apostolic ministry is as a
vanquished slave who is being led to his death by the con-
quering Christ; his life is to be consumed as an offering to his
victorious Lord. This is a position of extreme weakness/death
which paves the way for the triumph of God through the
power of the cross. Death gives way to life, and this,
according to Hafemann's reading of Paul, is the basis for a
truly apostolic ministry which follows the path of the
crucified Christ. The greatest strength of Hafemann's interpretation is the way in which it integrates the triumph
imagery of 2.14a and the sacrificial imagery of 2.14b-16a
within the wider argument of 2.14–4.6, and beyond that, sees

this theme of Paul's weakness as an apostle to be central to the Corinthian correspondence as a whole.

Finally, we note the suggestion made by P.B. Duff (1991) that behind Paul's use of the triumph image is a deliberate rhetorical strategy which is designed to counter any suspicions that the Corinthians might have had concerning Paul's financial dealings with them. Duff accepts that θριαμβεύειν was a military metaphor and that part of what Paul wished to convey to the Corinthians was embodied within it, but insists that a broader understanding of the metaphor is needed if we are to appreciate Paul's true intent. He suggests that θριαμβεύειν also has a rich association with epiphany processions of deities (such as Dionysus and Isis) in the ancient world, and that ideas associated with these religious celebrations are also part of what Paul meant to convey to the Corinthans by means of the metaphor. In order to move from the realm of the military triumph to that of the religious procession Duff suggests that in 2 Cor. 5.14a Paul expands the meaning of the military metaphor of 2.14 by the way in which he says (speaking of his apostolic ministry) that 'the love of Christ restrains us'. Crucial to Duff's case here is his interpretation of the essentially militaristic meaning of the verb 'restrains' (συνέχει) in 5.14, his suggestion being that Paul reinterprets the meaning of the metaphor of triumph with respect to his own apostolic ministry. As Duff puts it:

> He is a participant not in a military victory parade but in an epiphany procession. He has been captured, not as a prisoner of war, but as a devotee of a deity (p. 87).

Several other interesting allusions to the religious procession are identified by Duff in 2 Cor. 2.14–7.4, all of which are taken to support his basic contention. Included among these are: the mention of fragrant substances in 2.14-16, which are probably to be taken as cultic incense and thus more readily associated with a religious procession than with a military triumph; the mention of the vessels holding sacred objects of the cult in 4.7; and a structural parallel between 2.14 and 4.10 in which the apostle's public sufferings are associated with the epiphany processions of deity. Here several suggestions are pursued in which the metaphorical meaning of 'aroma' (εὐωδία) is enlarged to include cultic and religious dimensions of Paul's proclamation of the gospel. Having argued for all of these metaphorical expansions and associations, Duff then proceeds to apply them to the rhetorical strategy with which Paul began his apology in 2 Cor. 2.14. This is not unrelated to the interpretation of A.T. Hanson (1987, pp. 108-15), who discusses the relationship between 2 Cor. 2.14 and 1 Cor. 4.9-13, noting that the passages are illustrative of how in Paul's mind an essential function of apostleship is reproducing the sufferings of Christ within the life of the Church.

To return to P.B. Duff's argument for a moment: he suggests that Paul opens his letter in accordance with the classic canons of rhetorical advice, beginning his defence by taking up the theme of his rivals, namely accusations about his weakness and suffering and challenges about his right to call himself an apostle. Apparently Paul's opponents held a view of ministry which focused upon human victory and triumphalism. However, Paul quickly turns the metaphor of triumph to his own advantage (so Duff goes on to say) by adapting it, and reinterpreting it in accordance with the metaphor of epiphany processions well known in the Graeco-Roman world. The result of this rhetorical strategy is that the concerns and perceptions of the Corinthian church about the apostle are acknowledged, but that they are invited to enlarge their understanding and come to recognize that another way of viewing the situation is at hand.

'The Lord Is the Spirit' (3.17)

The interpretation of this phrase has long been a matter of debate, particularly as it so closely identifies 'the Lord' (ὁ κύριος) and 'the Spirit' (τὸ πνεῦμα). In addition, the place that 3.17 has in the overall argument of 3.12-18 is very difficult to determine. The tension here is so great that some interpreters have suggested removing the verse altogether, on the grounds that it is a post-Pauline interpolation, perhaps deriving from Gnostic circles. It is not surprising that the relationship of ὁ κύριος to τὸ πνεῦμα remains crucial to any interpretation of the passage, and most exegesis has focused

on this question. Many commentators take ὁ κύριος to refer to
Jesus Christ, although its precise relationship to the artic-
ular use of τὸ πνεῦμα remains a matter of considerable debate
and in the opinion of some calls into question this line of
interpretation. Alternatively, some commentators take ὁ
κύριος to refer to ˙Yahweh Himself, based upon a parallelism
of thought with 3.16a. Such an interpretation has the added
attraction of allowing a firm linkage of thought with 3.18b to
be established. Thus, the troublesome phrase in 3.18b
καθάπερ ἀπὸ κυρίου πνεύματος (with which Paul concludes the
chapter) can be paraphrased as, 'Such is the influence of the
Lord (Yahweh), who, after all, is present with us in the form
of the Spirit (of Christ)'. In the end, it may be impossible to
make a firm decision between the two possibilities, in that
the Spirit serves as the medium of the Christian's experience
of Christ, and through him, the experience of the living God
he represents.

'Embodying Death in the Midst of Life' (4.10)

2 Cor. 4.7-12 contains some of Paul's most profound declarations about the nature of Christian life and ministry. This
highly compressed passage is shot through with paradox and
contains several provocative, not to say unforgettable,
images. In 4.7 we have treasure juxtaposed with the earthen
vessels containing it; effectively this serves to contrast the
incomparable worth of the good news of salvation ('the treasure') with its embodiment in human beings ('the earthen
vessels'). Probably Paul has in mind here the 'treasure' of
apostolic ministry which he himself is privileged to embody
as a representative 'earthen vessel'. At the same time in 4.8-
9 we are presented with a set of four antitheses which are
highly structured and readily lend themselves to a poetic
phrasing such as that offered by J.B. Phillips: 'We are hard-
pressed on all sides, but we are never frustrated; we are
puzzled, but never in despair. We are persecuted, but are
never deserted: we may be knocked down but we are never
knocked out!' To top it off, there is in 4.10-12 a curious paragraph expounding the interplay between death and life; not
only is the death of Jesus portrayed as being made manifest
in *our* lives, but so too is *his* life being made manifest by *our*

death! (although Paul uses plural pronouns here it is clear he
has his own apostolic ministry primarily in mind).

Why does Paul use these images in 4.10-12? What is his
purpose in including them? Once again it is important to set
the context of this interesting passage in order to see his
point. Throughout 2 Cor. 2.14–7.14 Paul is engaged in
complex defence of his apostolic ministry, probably in response to a challenge made by his opponents in the church at
Corinth. Apparently there were some who interpreted Paul's
suffering and physical weakness as a sign of divine dis-
pleasure, if not punishment. The short paragraph in 4.10-12
is the most pointed rebuttal of such an interpretation of
human suffering. Within these verses Paul turns the tables
on his opponents and presents an alternative picture of his
apostolic sufferings, revealing their true place in the purposes of God. There is something of a theological dialectic in
operation here wherein God's values are contrasted with
those of human beings such as Paul. God's power is realized
in and through human suffering and weakness, and, as Paul's
own experience testifies, the true proclamation of the gospel
inevitably brings with it suffering and reproach. Here,
perhaps more clearly than anywhere else within the Pauline
letters, we are confronted with a Christ-centred theology of
suffering (cf. the 'word of the cross' in 1 Cor. 1.18). It is likely
that Paul saw the persecutions and hardships he had to
endure as an apostle as an extension of the humiliations and
sufferings that Jesus himself had to endure in his life; the
fourfold reference to 'Jesus' (to use his earthly name as
opposed to his Messianic title) in vv. 10-11 serves to indicate
this. It is also likely that Jesus' sufferings were earlier
alluded to in 1.5 where the evocative phrase 'the sufferings of
Christ' appears, and the similarity of vocabulary and expression between the two passages (1.5-7 and 4.10-12) leads one
to wonder if they share some common ground, perhaps in the
pre-Pauline tradition.

One of the most interesting considerations of this passage
concerns the use of the term 'death' (νέκρωσις) in 4.10a, a
word which appears only twice in the New Testament (the
other instance is in Rom. 4.19 in connection with the 'barren-
ness' of Sarah's womb). The term may even have been coined

by Paul, although it does appear in later Greek writers, notably the second-century physician Galen of Pergamum where it is used to describe the 'mortification' of bodies. There is some debate about whether the word means 'the state of death' or 'the process of dying', but most commentators agree with R.C. Tannehill (1967, p. 85) that νέκρωσις in 2 Cor. 4.10a is 'conceived as an active power at work in Paul's body'.

Another interesting consideration of 4.10b concerns the imagery underlying it, particularly the awkward phrase 'so that the life of Jesus may also be manifested in our bodies.' What is meant by this statement? P.B. Duff (1991) suggests that in 4.7-10 Paul is continuing the allusion to Graeco-Roman processions which he first used in 2.14-17 (see our discussion above). A connection of thought between the two passages is possible, given that 2.14 and 4.10 have several structural features in common (as Duff notes). However, the crucial verb 'to triumph' (θριαμβεύειν) from 2.14 is not used here in 4.10 and a connection of meaning between 'to triumph' and 'to make manifest' has to be inferred in order for the interpretation to work. However, Duff continues, the notion of 'carrying *around* (περιφέρων) the dying of Jesus' in 4.10a serves as a middle term and allows just such an inference to be drawn (the verb also occurs in 2.14 as well as again in 4.11). In short, Paul *may* be making use of imagery drawn from religious processions of the ancient world as part of his apostolic defence in 4.10, but it is difficult to see this as the primary image he has in mind, especially when we remember the essentially somatic nature of the verse. It is more likely that Paul has in mind Christ's physical crucifixion, and is thinking of the Lord having to bear (i.e. *carry* or *take up*) his cross. Or, perhaps Paul is ever conscious of his own bodily afflictions (hinted at in such passages as 2 Cor. 12.7 and Gal. 6.17) and alludes to his having to bear these as an apostle.

'Destruction of the Earthly Tent' (5.1-10)

In 4.16–5.10 we have one of the longest discussions about eschatological matters in the Pauline letters. Here Paul presents a montage of images: metaphors of buildings, garments, homes, as well as the basic anthropological contrast ('old humanity/new humanity'), are all used. However, it is important to recognize that 4.16–5.10 is not just an eschatological aside, but is an integral part of Paul's defence of his apostolic ministry running from 2.14–7.4. He is not so much simply sidetracked into discussing things to do with the future, but is setting any discussion of his apostleship within the bounds of his eschatological convictions. His ministry as an apostle is intimately tied up with his understanding of how the hope of the future impinges upon the certainties of the present. In short, within 4.16–5.10 we are looking again at what has often been described as 'realized eschatology' in Paul; his apostolic ministry is conducted 'between the times' with salvation already begun, but not yet consummated.

Nowhere is this eschatological tension more evident than in the 'heavenly house' metaphor Paul uses in 5.1, describing the believer as one who, although living now in an 'earthly tent', will one day be granted a resurrection body, a heavenly house 'not made with human hands (ἀχειροποίητον) which is eternal'. Although the primary idea here is that of the resurrected body of the *individual* believer, Paul's thinking has wider implications and it is possible to detect several corporate images converging. For example, it is easy to see an architectural image here, where the individual is portrayed as a constituent part, a 'brick', as it were, of the eternal temple of God. It is quite likely that the temple imagery used here ultimately comes from Jesus' own declarations about the temple made during his trial, notably Mk 14.58 where the same Greek word 'not made with human hands' (ἀχειροποίητον) appears on the lips of Jesus as a way of describing *his* resurrected body. Jesus' words here readily lent themselves to an ecclesiological interpretation wherein the church is described as his body, raised in glory. Similarly, Paul's Adamic Christology also contributes to the overall picture of the body of Christ with humankind's lost glory finding restoration in the person of the Second Adam, Jesus Christ.

The eschatological tension between present and future is expressed in several formal contrasts, notably in 5.1-8. Note the following:

Present	Future
earthly tent (5.1)	heavenly house (5.1)
capable of being destroyed (5.2)	eternal (5.1)
'naked' existence (5.3)	'clothed' existence (5.4)
mortal life (5.4)	immortal life (5.4)
home in the body (5.4)	home with the Lord (5.8)

Because the present earthly existence stands in such contrast to the future resurrection life, the believers 'groan and long to put on the heavenly dwelling' (5.2) and 'sigh with anxiety' (5.4).

There are many fascinating theological ideas which this passage opens up, including the possibility that Paul is here echoing a Corinthian slogan in 2 Cor. 5.6b. We shall have to restrict our discussion to two interrelated matters which have long occupied those who wrestle with Paul's words here: What did Paul believe would happen to believers at the consummation? Is he consistent when he presents this message of future hope? A host of exegetical problems arise from 2 Cor. 5.1-10, but none more difficult than the question of precisely what happens to the believer at death. How and when is the promise of the resurrection to be experienced? Does Paul here teach an 'intermediate state', where the deceased believer is present with God in a disembodied existence until the future parousia? It is sometimes suggested that Paul is moving away from the teaching found in 1 Corinthians 15 in the direction of a more gnostic understanding of the resurrection body as something which is *exchanged for* rather than something which is *put on* over the physical body. A good deal hinges here on how much should be made of the difference between the two verbs ἐνδύσασθαι and ἐπενδύσασθαι, both of which convey the idea of getting dressed. In short, the suggestion is that believers who are alive at the parousia might be said to 'put on' the resurrection body without 'putting off' their mortal bodies; they experience transformation without the 'destruction of the earthly tent'.

On this basis some have argued that 2 Cor. 5.1-10 indicates a significant development in Paul's thinking about the nature of the bodily resurrection, perhaps even an abandonment of it altogether. Because 5.1-10 seems to reflect a

dualism of body and spirit, which was so characteristic of
Hellenistic thought, it is sometimes said to stand in contrast
to 1 Corinthians 15 which is much more within the tradition
of Hebraic thought and presents the future resurrection as a
unity of body and spirit. Whether or not Paul expected his
own literal transformation into the glorified resurrection
body at the parousia of Christ is a question which lies at the
heart of the debate about these two passages. Did Paul
believe he would die before the parousia or not? Is the resurrection to take place at the coming of Christ or is it to take
place at the death of the believer? C.H. Dodd (1953) is
perhaps one of the best known advocates of an interpretation
of Paul which sees a fundamental shift to have occurred in
the apostle's thought on the subject of his own mortality.
Dodd suggests that a brush with death, which occurred
between the writing of 1 Corinthians and 2 Corinthians, has
forced a revolution in Paul's mind on these matters and that
we see this reflected in the letters themselves. Others
disagree with this way of setting 2 Cor. 5.1-10 over against
1 Corinthians 15 and instead detect a continuity in Paul's
thought here. The matter has been the subject of considerable debate and several detailed studies comparing the two
passages have been produced. Much depends on how one
defines 'development', as opposed to a difference of emphasis,
within Paul's thought. To widen the horizons somewhat, we
could say that what is being hammered out in much of this
scholarly debate concerns the relationship between the
Hellenistic world and the world of Judaism, and, more
importantly, where Paul is thought to fit within the two. As
long as the debate about the relationship between Hellenism
and Judaism rages 2 Cor. 5.1-10 will continue to be a focal
text; and as long as interest in personal immortality remains
a preoccupation for people Paul's words here will continue
both to fascinate, and to fox, the reader.

'Knowing Christ according to the Flesh' (5.16)

So difficult is this verse to interpret, and so unusual is it
within the bounds of Pauline thought, that it has been taken
by some to be a later Gnostic gloss. W. Schmithals (1971,
pp. 302-15) is the classic advocate of such an approach,

arguing that 5.16 interrupts the flow of Paul's thought in
5.11-15 and 5.17 (a section which is part of Paul's defence of
his apostolic ministry running from 2.14–7.4). He suggests
that 5.16 was inserted by one of Paul's Corinthian opponents
to support the Gnostic belief that the earthly person of Jesus
was to be despised as a temporary dwelling place for the
heavenly redeemer. This interpolation theory is confirmed, so
he continues, by the presence of 'so that' (ὥστε) with which
5.17 begins; the connective word forges a link with the
preceding thought of 5.14-15 and highlights the interpolation
of 5.16 in the process. J. O'Neill (1987) also concentrates on
the difficulties that 5.16 presents in the overall argument of
5.14-20 and proposes a similar solution. He takes the reference to 'Christ' in 5.16 to be a later Docetic gloss. When this
gloss is removed, so he says, the passage flows much more
smoothly and the sense of the verse becomes: 'we no longer
regard people according to their outward appearance: if we
had once done so, we do so no longer'.

Debate about the meaning of this cryptic verse hinges
upon the meaning of the twofold use of 'according to the flesh'
(κατὰ σάρκα). The expression can mean a variety of things in
Paul's thought (it occurs some 19 times). It is used simply to
denote a family genealogy (as in Rom. 1.3; 4.1; 9.3, 5; 1 Cor.
10.18; cf. Eph. 6.5 and Col. 3.22) and it is used as an allegori-
cal image (as in Gal. 4.23, 29). Above all, the phrase is used
in an ethical sense, that is, as an expression of action which
is motivated by human, even carnal, desires (as in Rom. 8.4,
13; 1 Cor. 1.26; 2 Cor. 1.17; 10.2-3; 11.18). The ethical sense
of the phrase also seems indicated in 2 Cor. 10.3, where an
interesting contrast is set up between 'according to the flesh'
(κατὰ σάρκα) and 'in the flesh' (ἐν σαρκί), a contrast which,
unfortunately, is somewhat lost by the rendering of the RSV:
'though we live in the world we are not carrying on a worldly
war'.

The diversity of meaning that κατὰ σάρκα can bear in
2 Cor. 5.16 is reflected in the range of translations offered
for the phrase. Both the RSV and the nrsv translate it as 'from
a human point of view'; the NIV renders it as 'according to
worldly standards'; the NAB gives 'in terms of human judgment'; the JB 'in the flesh'; Moffatt 'what is external'; J.B.

Phillips 'as a man'; and M. Dibelius and W.G. Kümmel (1953, p. 66) take the relevant clause 'we regard no one from a human point of view' to mean 'we completely abandon all reliance on human relationships'. F.C. Porter (1928, p. 269) even offers the intriguing suggestion that the phrase here is best rendered 'selfishly', a translation which goes far in resolving many of the theological difficulties of the passage.

Almost all commentators agree that the two halves of the verse are parallel to each other, that the truth expressed in v. 16b is in some way to be understood as related to the assertion in v. 16a. However, the focus of much of the exegetical debate on the verse centres on two difficult points of Greek grammar. The first concerns the fact that v. 16b is a conditional statement introduced by the words εἰ καί, which is generally rendered 'if we once regarded Christ from a human point of view...' The question here is whether this is meant to be taken as a hypothetical case, designed to make the reality of the first part of the verse more clear by contrast. The sense of the phrase would then be 'even if we once regarded Christ from a human point of view (although we did not actually do so)...' However, many others insist that the natural sense of the Greek words is to introduce a real condition, indicating an opinion which had actually been held by some (perhaps even including Paul) in the past. Thus it is better to take v. 16b to mean, 'even though we once regarded Christ from a human point of view...'

Secondly, much of the nub of the exegetical debate hinges on whether κατὰ σάρκα is to be taken adverbially, modifying the two verbs translated as 'to know', or whether it is to be taken adjectivally, modifying the nouns 'no one' and 'Christ' (assuming, of course, that the two halves of the verse are intended as parallels). If the latter possibility is followed (that 'according to the flesh' modifies the nouns of the sentence), the verse can be taken to mean that Paul no longer has any interest in the historical person of Jesus of Nazareth, even though he may have held such an interest in the past. However, R. Bultmann (1985, p. 154) insists that the adverbial/adjectival debate is something of an artificial distinction, since 'to know people as they are met in the world means also to know them in worldly fashion'. At the

same time Bultmann has, throughout the course of his long
career, consistently challenged oft-asserted interpretations of
the phrase as expressive of Paul's interest in, or perhaps
even acquaintance with, the historical Jesus. Instead, he
argues that Paul was really interested only in the believer's
existential encounter with the exalted Lord. Thus he
comments on the critical verse:

> For Paul, Christ has lost his identity as an individual human
> person. He knows him no longer 'after the flesh' (2 Cor. 5.16).
> Instead, Jesus has become a cosmic figure, a body to which all
> belong who have been joined to him through faith and baptism
> (1956, p. 197).

Such an interpretation is typical of a number of exegetes,
particularly German scholars following in the tradition of the
Tübingen school. However, many would challenge such negative assessments of the historical person of Jesus in favour of
an exalted cosmic Christ. G.R. Beasley-Murray goes so far as
to state:

> It is a monstrous interpretation of the apostle's words to imagine
> that they were intended to convey a lack of interest in the 'Christ
> according to the flesh,' as though he had no time for Jesus of
> Nazareth, only the Christ of heaven (1971, p. 41).

Feelings certainly run high when it comes to the question
of the place that the historical Jesus held within Paul's
thought. While it is improbable, on the basis of 2 Cor. 5.16
alone, that one can insist that Paul did indeed meet Jesus of
Nazareth prior to his experience on the road to Damascus
(perhaps when both were in Jerusalem?), a denial of such
knowledge by the apostle hardly seems the real meaning of
the verse. If nothing else, the fact that Paul opens the controversial clause in 5.16b with a plural pronoun ('if *we* regarded
Christ according to the flesh') renders this interpretation
extremely suspect.

It is more probable that the opinion which Paul regards as
inadequate, the thing which he came to regard as unaccept-
able and described as 'knowing Jesus after the flesh', is tied
up with his pre-Christian understanding of Jesus as the
messiah. Paul, so the argument goes, came to realize that his
pre-conversion conception of the messiah was faulty, that it
needed to be tempered with the awful truth of Jesus Christ's

suffering and death on the cross which eventually gave way to his vindication and exaltation. In other words, a restrictive Jewish nationalism is to be rejected in the light of what God has brought about in Christ. Probably Paul had in mind his own conversion experience as the decisive point of transition, the event which separates what was 'before' from what is 'now'.

We are driven by the sheer weight of the theological imagery Paul employs in 5.16 to see beyond a simplistic contrast between the historical Jesus and the exalted Lord. Thus F.W. Danker (1989), who takes the phrase κατὰ σάρκα to be an adverbial expression, associates the verb 'to know' with the change of perspective brought about by the 'new creation' (καινὴ κτίσις) which has been wrought through the death and resurrection of Christ (5.17). This is similar to the opinion of J.L. Martyn (1967) who stresses the transition between two ages implied by the phrases 'no longer' (μηκέτι), 'from now on' (ἀπὸ τοῦ νῦν) and 'no longer' (νῦν οὐκέτι) in 2 Cor. 5.15-16, a transition which he says is made real by the death and resurrection of Jesus Christ. This means, in Martyn's opinion, that for Paul the contrast to knowledge 'according to the flesh' is not knowledge 'in the spirit', but rather knowledge 'according to the cross'. G.N. Stanton similarly puts his finger on the essence of the matter when he says:

> The main point of 2 Cor. 5.16 is clear: as a consequence of the death and resurrection of Jesus, Christians have a new perspective on all things and all people and no longer 'know' κατὰ σάρκα (1974, p. 93).

'He Who Knew No Sin' (5.21)

M.D. Hooker has made this critical verse the object of special investigation during her long and distinguished career, identifying it as a central plank of what she calls Paul's theology of 'interchange'. She aptly describes 2 Cor. 5.21 as one of the two most difficult statements contained within Paul's letters, the other being Gal. 3.13 (1990, p. 13). Several features of 5.21, and the paragraph in which it is set (5.14-21), make it problematic. First, there is the matter of determining the

overall context of the passage within the letter. In 5.14-21
Paul is continuing a spirited defence of his apostolic
ministry, responding to challenges made against him by
opponents in the church at Corinth. Within this apology he
emphasizes his call to be an agent of reconciliation in the
ongoing redemptive activity of God in Christ (v. 18), and
concludes the paragraph with a stunning declaration about
'God making him (Christ) sin' (v. 21). What of the structure
and line of argument within these verses? A number of
suggestions have been proposed. It is perhaps best to take
the two parts of vv. 18 and 19 as parallels in thought. Thus,
the sense of v. 18a ('God reconciled us to Himself through
Christ') is echoed in v. 19a ('God was in Christ reconciling the
world to Himself, not counting their trespasses against
them'), while the meaning of v. 18b ('God gave us the ministry of reconciliation') has its counterpart in v. 19b ('God
entrusts us with the message of reconciliation'). There are
two basic ideas here: the first focuses on what God has done
for us in initiating reconciliation, and the second focuses on
what we as reconciled people are to do as a result. These
same two key ideas are picked up in 5.20-21, but here they
are put in reverse order. Thus, 5.20 ('we are ambassadors for
Christ...') describes the Christian's responsibility to be a
reconciling agent in the world, and 5.21 ('God made him to be
sin...') provides yet another declaration of God's action in
providing reconciliation for us, but this time filling it out
more by using sacrificial imagery drawn from the Old
Testament (more on this below). In short, it is clear that
apostleship and reconciliation are intimately linked in Paul's
mind and that the two ideas help define the nature of
ministry for him. Indeed, it is possible to argue that the
doctrine of reconciliation is foundational to the whole of
Paul's theology, providing a place where his ideas of
justification by faith, of salvation, his ecclesiology and his
eschatology all intersect. Here in 2 Corinthians 5, however, it
is to defend his apostolic calling as 'the apostle to the
Gentiles' that he writes these words to the Corinthians.
Many argue that throughout 5.14-21 Paul is identifying
himself with the servant of the servant-songs of Deutero-
Isaiah, particularly as a means of expressing his under-

standing of his call to minister among the Gentile nations (the quotation of Isa. 49.8-9 in 2 Cor. 6.2 also supports this suggestion).

Secondly, there is the question of the vocabulary that Paul uses here, notably the use of 'reconciliation' language in 5.14, 18-20. Some statistical evidence will help to illustrate the point. The Greek noun translated as 'reconciliation' (καταλλαγή) occurs four times in Paul's letters (Rom. 5.11; 11.15; 2 Cor. 5.18, 19), but nowhere else in the New Testament. Meanwhile, there are two verbs rendered 'to reconcile' in the Pauline letters, both of which are linguistically related to the noun καταλλαγή. The first verb (καταλλάσσειν) occurs six times in Paul (Rom. 5.10a, b; 1 Cor. 7.11; 2 Cor. 5.18, 19, 20), but, again, nowhere else in the New Testament. The second verb (ἀποκαταλλάσσειν) appears four times, always in the Pauline letters (1 Cor. 7.1; Eph. 2.16; Col. 1.20, 22). It has been suggested that the verb ἀποκαταλλάσσειν was invented by Paul since it is unattested in literature earlier than the New Testament. It is also noteworthy that God is almost always the subject of the two verbs concerned; the only exception occurs in 1 Cor. 7.11 where it is stated that a divorced woman should remain single if separated (divorced?) from her husband, or else 'be reconciled' (καταλλαγήτω) to him. T.W. Manson (1963) summarizes the essential point well when he says 'reconciliation is thus a one-sided transaction. God reconciles; man is reconciled' (p. 51).

The striking thing to notice from all this is that 'reconciliation' language is exclusively Pauline, and predominantly theocentric. The fact that Paul chose to employ this terminology as a means of explaining the Christian message, when no one else in the New Testament did so, suggests that it was particularly meaningful to him. The theme of reconciliation lies at the heart of 5.14-21, one of the most theologically profound declarations in all of the Pauline corpus. At the same time, 'reconciliation' is an idea which is particularly relevant for the contemporary reader. As W. Baird says:

> Of all Paul's metaphors of salvation, reconciliation may be the easiest for moderns to appreciate, and therefore, the most fruitful for preaching. The terms 'reconcile' and 'reconciliation' can be used

for personal relationships which are common to our experience
(1980, p. 87).

Herein lies the nub of the problem, however. What exactly do
'reconcile' and 'reconciliation' mean? The basic meaning of
the words in Greek is 'to make other' or 'change', and
etymologically they are related to the root αλλ- meaning
'other'. About this there is general agreement. However the
question becomes: How is such change brought about? What
is it that brings about this 'otherness'? Such questions lead
us to consider next the Old Testament background of the
idea of reconciliation, particularly the sacrificial imagery
which is often said to be at its heart.

It is important to note that Paul does not say 'God made
him (Christ) a sinner', but 'God made him sin'. This has the
effect of emphasizing the sinlessness of Jesus within the
redemptive purposes of God while simultaneously inviting a
rather literal interpretation of his death as a sacrifice. Thus,
R. Bultmann comments on 'made him sin' in 5.21:

> The meaning is, just as believers are 'just' because God regards
> ('reckons') and treats them as such, though they are sinners, so
> Christ is regarded and treated by God as a sinner (1985, p. 165).

The key point is that although Jesus was sinless, God treats
him as a sinner by allowing him to die an ignominious death
on the cross. Debate has long raged over whether or not the
use of the word 'sin' (ἁμαρτίαν) in 5.21 means that Christ is
being equated with the 'sin-offering' frequently found in Old
Testament texts (such as Lev. 4.24-26; 5.12; 6.17; Num. 6.14;
8.8; and Ps. 40.6) which speak of ritual sacrifice. This debate
is reflected in the difficulties that many modern translations
have in rendering the verse. Paul's language is very compressed and needs to be expanded before we are to grasp the
theological meaning of the verse as a whole. We could
express these expansions with a translation such as 'For our
sake God made him, who did not know any *guilt on account
of* sin, to be *an atoning offering for* sin in order that we might
become *people who exhibit* the righteousness of God'.

However, whether or not we concede that such sacrificial
imagery lies behind Paul's declaration in 5.21, we are still
left with the difficult task of explaining what Christ's
sacrificial death means theologically. This prompts a

consideration of how sacrifice relates to the atonement, and beyond that how both are connected to Paul's wider theme of reconciliation. Several so-called 'theories of atonement' have been suggested over the years. They all attempt to explain the significance of Christ's death on the cross and what kind of relationship he had to humankind through that death. The key term here is 'relationship', for reconciliation is above all a relational, as opposed to a forensic or financial, concept; it explores the change of relationship between parties rather than the *mechanism* of that change. Thus a distinction should be made between the *reconciliation* of God and humankind brought about by Christ's atoning death, and *expiation* or *propitiation* as theological explanations of the legalities (who paid what to whom and why?) which are implicit within that death.

A common way to interpret Christ's death is to describe it as either *substitutionary* or *representational* in nature; 2 Cor. 5.21 has been taken to support both interpretations. In addition to 2 Cor. 5.21 there are two other passages where Paul makes similar reference to Christ's death, namely Rom. 8.3-4 and Gal. 3.13. Indeed, D.E.H. Whiteley (1957, p. 244) describes these three passages as the 'foundation stones of the substitutionary theory'.

Most agree that Christ's death was in some sense substitutionary, but how so? What sort of legal transaction, if any, is implied by the substitution? Should we understand it to be *penal* substitution, and if so, to whom was the penalty paid? The parallel passages in Rom. 8.3-4 and Gal. 3.13 are often cited by those who see Christ's death as a penalty for sin. The latter passage is particularly important in that it says that Christ became a *curse*, paralleling his being made *sin* in 2 Cor. 5.21. Gal. 3.13 is often regarded as a pre-Pauline formulation of the significance of Christ's death, probably arising out of a Jewish-Christian setting (hence the unusual citation from Deut. 21.23). Similarly, E. Käsemann (1971, p. 52) suggests that Paul is drawing upon a Jewish-Christian hymnic tradition in 2 Cor. 5.19-21. But do we have any hints about the *source* of this pre-Pauline material? There are some important antecedents, most notably the interesting use of the verb καταλλάσσειν in 2 Macc. 7.30-38 where the martyrdom of seven brothers at the hands of the evil ruler Antiochus is presented as a redemptive act for the nation Israel. Clearly the brothers' death is substitutionary in that they ask God to accept their deaths on behalf of the nation. It is often suggested that the Hellenistic-Jewish formulation of the Pauline passage, heavily dependent as it is on Old Testament ideas of sacrifice and atonement, points to an origin in Jerusalem or in Judaea. P. Stuhlmacher (1986, pp. 58-60) identifies the origin more specifically, suggesting that it reflects the theology of either the Stephen-circle in Jerusalem, or perhaps that of the church in Antioch which was comprised largely of the Hellenists from Judaea who were driven out of Jerusalem following Stephen's martyrdom. In any case, the tradition (so Stuhlmacher argues) bears striking similarities to the self-understanding of Jesus himself for whom the Suffering Servant motif was all-important. A strong note of continuity between Jesus and Paul is sounded by such a suggestion. On the other hand, others downplay the pre-Pauline angle and stress Paul's own originality in 5.14-21, focusing on the creative use of 'reconciliation' language in the passage.

The reference in 2 Cor. 5.14 to Christ's death 'for all' (ὑπὲρ πάντων) is also important and again may point to the Old Testament suffering servant motif (the related Greek word translated as 'many' or 'all' [πολλοί] appears five times in the LXX of Isa. 52.13-53.12, for example). But what does Christ's death 'for all' mean here? Is ὑπέρ ('for' or 'on behalf of') the equivalent of ἀντί ('as a substitute for' or 'in the place of')? Does Christ die *as a substitute for* or *as a representative of* the faithful? Both cases have been vigorously defended. Most now agree that ὑπέρ stresses *representation*, while ἀντί stresses *substitution*. This subtle, but theologically significant, distinction takes us once again to the heart of the debate about the meaning of 2 Cor. 5.21. Paul clearly did understand Jesus Christ to be, at least in some sense, a representative figure; the portrayal of him as a second Adam (Rom. 5.12-21; 1 Cor. 15.20-22; 15.45-49) leaves no doubt of that. Thus, 2 Cor. 5.14 contrasts the death of Jesus with the death of the humankind he represents: 'we are convinced that one has died for all; therefore all have died'. Yet it is difficult to deny that Paul also uses the language of sacrifice when he goes on to expound the significance of Jesus's death in 5.20-21. Consequently, we should not set the idea of representation over against the idea of sacrificial substitution, and try to force a distinction upon Paul's thought. As J.D.G. Dunn puts it:

> to say that Jesus died as a representative of fallen man and to say that Jesus died as a sacrifice for the sins of men is for Paul to say the same thing (1974, p. 137).

It may well be that the significance of the death of Jesus was so great, and the wonder of it so beyond anything imagined, that both concepts, representation and sacrificial substitution, were needed to try and express it. This is not to say that either concept plumbs the depths of theological truth, or even that the two concepts together can do so, but together they allow us to begin to wrestle with the centrality of Jesus's death in Paul's thought. In short, the language of representation and the language of substitution merge at the cross. Perhaps we need to try and communicate this merging by using yet another term to describe the meaning of Christ's death: it was an act of *identification*. The translation of 5.21 offered by H.W. Cassirer (*God's New Covenant: A New Testament Translation* [Grand Rapids: Eerdmans, 1989]). brings this point out well: 'For our sake he made him who was a stranger to sin become one with human sinfulness, so that, united to him, the very righteousness of God might become ours'.

A related issue is also raised within 5.14-21, namely the role that God has in the redemptive act. Clearly God is the prime mover within the act of redemption. He is the initiator, rather than simply the recipient of the redemptive act of Christ 'on behalf of many'. This is not to say that human beings have no part to play in the drama of redemption; they clearly do. However, the stress that Paul lays on God's role in the matter ('*God* was in Christ reconciling the world to Himself'—the positioning of the Greek is emphatic) serves to set up a proper relationship between divine initiative and human response. At the same time, the passage is unashamedly christological. The redeeming action by God is described in 5.14 as an expression of 'the love of *Christ*' (= ἀγάπη τοῦ

Χριστοῦ), an unusual phrase occurring elsewhere in the undisputed letters of Paul only in Rom. 8.35 (cf. Eph. 3.19 and 5.14). However, we should not think of Christ standing between God and humankind in the act of reconciliation; that is too adversarial a picture and sets Christ over against God. Rather, God is the active force in the drama of redemption and he is working through Christ. Given the divine initiative in salvation, another point for consideration arises. How wide are the redemptive purposes of God? Should 5.19-21 be viewed as an expression of the cosmic purposes of God, so that the whole of the created order is involved in the reconciliation described (as Käsemann 1971 suggests)? Col. 1.20 does, after all, describe reconciliation in just such terms, for the author speaks of God reconciling 'all things, whether on earth or in heaven'. There may be some grounds for seeing reconciliation as extending beyond the Corinthians themselves, especially when we remember Paul's wide-ranging missionary interests and his stated desire to take the message of the gospel to the furthest reaches of the known world (i.e. Spain). Is there a sense in which reconciliation might be seen as a cosmic event for Paul? J. Koenig (1990) offers an intriguing suggestion precisely along these lines. Although not necessarily accepting E. Käsemann's influential ideas about a gnostic myth of cosmic redemption underlying the passage, he suggests that in 5.20 Paul is not so much concerned with the reconciliation of the *Corinthians* to God, as with the reconciliation of the *world* to God. He points out that first-person plural pronouns can often have an inclusive sense, and uses this as a basis for widening the scope of reconciliation, at least as far as our reading of Paul is concerned. Thus, the meaning of the verse is: 'So all of us believers are ambassadors for Christ, God making his appeal through us. We are beseeching [the world] on Christ's behalf, "You [world], be reconciled to God".' Of course, how far Paul's understanding of 'world' remained essentially anthropological is left open. But there appears to be no doubt in Paul's mind that reconciliation carries with it a certain responsibility. As C.B. Cousar (1981, p. 183) puts it: 'To be reconciled means also to be reconciling'.

One further point is worth mentioning here. M.D. Hooker (1990, p. 22) calls attention to the oft-cited passage from Irenaeus's *Adversus Haer.* 5 as a parallel to Paul's declaration in 5.14-21. 'He became what we are that we might become what he is'. She suggests, however, that Paul's thought has an additional element which Irenaeus's does not. Paul goes on to define in christological terms the *place* where 'we become what he is'. Although Paul does not actually write in 5.21, 'God made him to be sin in order that *in him* we might become the righteousness of God', that appears to be the logic of his thought. Some question this idea, however, on the grounds that it brings a different focus to the meaning of 'righteousness of God' than is found elsewhere in Paul's letters, notably Rom. 1.17; 3.21, 25; and 10.3. Instead of the normal stress on the divine dimension ('the righteousness of *God*') we have here the human dimension coming to the fore ('*we* become the righteousness of God [in him]'). Admittedly, the phrase is awkward; nowhere else does Paul speak of human beings *becoming* the righteousness of God. On the other hand, it may well be that Paul is here using traditional material and this is itself responsible for this shift in focus.

Finally, there is the question of *when* it is that this act of reconciliation takes place. At what point in Jesus' life does God 'make him to be sin'? Is it at his incarnation or at his death? Does Christ become sin when he is born or is it when he dies on the cross? Paul does not address this question explicitly and perhaps we should not try to decide between the two events of Christ's life. The point for Paul is that Jesus Christ so identified with humankind through becoming a man that he was able to effect reconciliation through his death on the cross. In short, incarnation and crucifixion are best viewed together, both demonstrating Christ's identification with humankind.

'The One who Did the Wrong' (7.12)

The identity of the offender alluded to in 2 Cor. 7.12 has long been a matter of considerable dispute. It has invariably been tied up with discussions of both 2 Cor. 2.5-11 and 1 Cor. 5.1-5, and is generally linked to larger discussions about the identity of the opponents Paul is facing in 2 Corinthians. In

part, any resolution of this mystery depends on how one
views 2 Corinthians 1–9 fitting with 2 Corinthians 10–13,
and beyond that, how both fit together with 1 Corinthians.
Questions about whether the offender was a member of the
Corinthian congregation (and therefore subject to the discipline of the church) have also been raised. Both possibilities
have been argued: thus C.K. Barrett (1982, pp. 108-17) takes
the offender to be an outsider who was closely associated
with the church in Corinth, while G. Lüdemann (1989, pp.
81-82) takes him to have been a Gentile Corinthian
Christian.

Another key question is whether Paul himself was the one
who was offended against, the τοῦ ἀδικηθέντος of 2 Cor. 7.12,
or whether the one offended against might refer to Paul's
representative in Corinth, perhaps Titus or Timothy.
Suggestions that Timothy might be indicated seem to run
aground on the way Paul alludes to the personal anguish he
suffered in visiting the Corinthians (2 Cor. 2.1; cf. 2 Cor. 1.1,
13). Most recent commentators accept Paul as the one who
has been offended against, although Timothy, and even Titus,
are occasionally put forward as alternative possibilities.

Most who accept the canonical order of the Corinthian
letters (and their essential integrity) have followed the
Church's traditional interpretation and sought to establish
the identity of the offender of 7.12 as the incestuous man
referred to in 1 Cor. 5.1-5 and, presumably, the offended as
his father. Such an identification usually proceeds in three
steps: first, an equation of the offender of 2 Cor. 7.12 and the
offender of 2 Cor. 2.5-11 is made; secondly, an equation of the
letter Paul wrote in which he discusses the matter (alluded
to in 2 Cor. 5.9) and the canonical 1 Corinthians is made;
thirdly, assuming that 1 Corinthians is the letter alluded to
in 2 Cor. 5.9, it is only natural to take the incident in 1 Cor.
5.1-5 to refer to the same offender (the references to Satan in
1 Cor. 5.5 and 2 Cor. 2.11 are also seen to support the
identification of a single person as ultimately responsible for
the problems addressed by Paul in all three passages). It is to
be noted that this interpretation assumes not only that Paul
made a visit to Corinth prior to the writing of the 'painful
letter', but that Paul's letter (mentioned in 2 Cor. 2.3-4) is

our canonical 1 Corinthians—an assumption many scholars are unwilling to concede.

Perhaps the most weighty point against this interpretation is the fact that the offence alluded to in 2 Cor. 2.5-11 (and 2 Cor. 7.12) does not seem to have been the specific act of sexual misconduct suggested by 1 Cor. 5.1-5, but a more directed attack against the person and authority of Paul himself. Other inconsistencies also make the traditional solution problematic, including the sanctions which are levied on the incestuous man in 1 Cor. 5.1-5 and the unknown opponent of 2 Corinthians 2 and 7. In short, it is difficult to see the church discipline imposed upon the man in 2 Cor. 2.6-7 as anything like as serious as the 'handing over to Satan' mentioned in 1 Cor. 5.5. Yet something of a compromise has been reached by C. Kruse (1987, 1988, 1989) who, while taking due note of some of the tensions between 1 Corinthians 5 and 2 Corinthians 2 and 7, maintains that the offender in both letters is one and the same person. In order to do this, Kruse suggests that the incestuous man of 1 Cor. 5.1-5 committed an additional offence against Paul, probably when the apostle was in Corinth for his second (unrecorded) visit. In short, Paul's attempt to bring the offender to church discipline was not firmly backed by the church and an inevitable rift ensued. This gave rise to Paul's return to Ephesus and his later description of the time spent with the Corinthians as his 'painful visit' (2 Cor. 2.1). It may well be, Kruse speculates, that one of the reasons for the reluctance of the church to support Paul in the matter was a growing sense of general uncertainty about his apostleship (brought on by the arrival of Peter in Corinth?). One of the great strengths of this interpretation is that it takes the opposition reflected in 2 Corinthians 1–7 and that reflected in 10–13 ultimately to be generated by the same person, namely the incestuous man. However, one of the weaknesses of this interpretation is the lack of insight it has to offer about what it was that the offender (as opposed to those who used the situation to denigrate Paul) actually did as a follow-up to his incest which so antagonized Paul and resulted in a split within the church.

However, M.E. Thrall (1987) has recently suggested a different solution to the identification of the offender, one

which builds precisely on a novel understanding of the
nature of the offence itself which was committed against
Paul (or his representative). I mention her interpretation
here in some detail, if for no other reason than to show how
ingenuity can be applied in an attempt to solve the enigma of
2 Cor. 7.12. Thrall calls attention to the vague reference to
legal proceedings in 1 Cor. 6.7-8 and suggests that Paul was
accused of impropriety with regard to business matters,
involving money or property, and that this was the substance
of the accusation(s) made against him by an unnamed individual. She goes on (quite fancifully!) to surmise that one
member of the congregation at Corinth entrusted Paul with
money which was to be put toward the collection for
Jerusalem. This money was stolen from Paul, probably by
another member of the congregation, and the matter was
brought before the whole church. Because it was very much a
matter of one person's word against another's, the church did
not know how to act decisively in the matter, which led Paul
to assume that they were unsupportive of him and questioned his integrity. Unable to remain in such an atmosphere
of suspicion and doubt, Paul hurried off back to Ephesus from
whence he wrote the (missing) 'painful' letter mentioned in
2 Cor. 2.3-4. In the meantime, the leaders at Corinth investi-
gated the matter more fully and arrived at the truth,
confirming Paul's version of the events, obtaining the
offender's confession of the theft, and instituting suitable
punishment by the church. Needless to say, Thrall's theory is
not supported by much solid evidence in the text; conjecture
upon conjecture is needed to sustain her argument, and that
is its greatest weakness. It does, however, add another novel
scenario to the number of hypothetical reconstructions of
who Paul was fighting against in Corinth and why. In the
process it does offer a framework in which to understand
many of the innuendoes and subtleties contained within
2 Corinthians. Alas, in the end, we are forced to admit that
the identity of the opponent alluded to in 2 Cor. 7.12 remains
a mystery. V.P. Furnish's summary of the incident is about
as far as it is possible to go without tipping over into pure
speculation:

Paul had been slandered, probably to his face, by an unnamed
individual. A majority of the Corinthian congregation had agreed
to some sort of disciplinary action against him, but only after the
seriousness and wider meaning of the offense had been brought
home to it by Paul's tearful letter. Confident now of the church's
obedience, he writes again about the matter, this time urging that
the offending party be forgiven and brought back into the
Christian community (1984, p. 168).

'Caught up to the Third Heaven' (12.2)

In 2 Cor. 12.1-10 Paul gives us a provocative picture of a
heavenly journey. He couches the story in veiled terms,
narrating it in the third person, and there has been some
debate about whether this is a heavenly journey of Paul
himself or the experience of someone else known to him.
Most commentators agree that Paul is speaking of himself
here. It could be that this style of detached narration is a
sign of humility on Paul's part, or, to take another equally
plausible angle on the matter, that it is a deliberate use of
irony by him in which he contrasts his experience with those
claimed by his opponents. Thus Paul appeals to heavenly
visions and divine revelations as part of his strategy to challenge his opponents who ridicule him as unimpressive and
unspectacular. This makes sense of the unusual reference to
'fourteen years' in 12.2; it is a way of stressing that his
visionary experience pre-dates that of his opponents. The fact
that Paul uses plurals in 12.1, 7, describing 'visions and revelations of the Lord' and the 'abundance of revelations'
suggests that Paul had more than just the one experience
fourteen years ago. Rather, such experiences were a regular
part of his religious experience; we might even call him a
'visionary' or an 'ecstatic'. It is possible to identify no less
than eight or so visions associated with the ministry of Paul,
although most of them occur in stories recorded in Acts,
including the three accounts of Paul's Damascus Road
encounter (9.1-19; 22.4-16; 26.12-18). However, is the heavenly journey described in 2 Cor. 12.1-10 the same as Paul's
vision on the Damascus Road (mentioned in Gal. 1.11-17;
1 Cor. 9.1; 15.5-8) in which the risen Lord Jesus calls
him into service as an apostle? Almost certainly not,

although there are some points of similarity between the two experiences. The heavenly journey motif is well known in Jewish writings, both in the traditions of apocalyptic literature and in mystical literature focusing on the vision of the throne-chariot contained in Ezekiel 1. The latter is sometimes known as *merkabah* mysticism because of the place that the *merkabah* (the Hebrew word for 'chariot') has within the heavenly visions. The importance of this strand of Jewish religious experience for the New Testament era is now widely recognized and it is generally accepted that Paul's presentation of the meaning of the gospel owes much to Jewish apocalyptic traditions. Consequently, there have been a number of studies in recent years in which Jewish descriptions of heavenly journeys have been compared with 2 Cor. 12.1-10. However, the suggestion that Paul's vision derives directly from the tradition of *merkabah* mysticism has been particularly contentious, with some asserting and others denying such a connection. Two features of Paul's description which tie in quite well with other Jewish accounts of heavenly ascents are the description of the various levels of heaven and the mention of the destination of the journey as 'paradise'. Both ideas are regularly found in Jewish works, the most famous being *2 Enoch*. We can safely assume that for Paul being 'caught up to the third heaven' in 12.2 and being 'caught up into paradise' in 12.3 refer to the same experience (the same Greek verb is used in both phrases). He is describing a single ascent, not two successive stages of his heavenly journey.

The fact that the mysteries revealed to Paul while in the heavenly paradise are 'unutterable words' (ἄρρητα ῥήματα) is somewhat odd. Usually the contents of such heavenly journeys are described in terms of things that are *seen*, not things that are *heard*. Perhaps not too much should be made of this, however, since Paul regularly employs visual terms and categories when he describes other visions he has had. Paul chooses here to describe his heavenly vision as revealing to him 'things that cannot be told, which man may not utter' in order to set himself over against his opponents in Corinth who magnified their ecstatic experiences and (if the problems over *glossolalia* in 1 Corinthians are anything to go by) made too much of a public show of it all. In short, much of the interpretation of the heavenly journey depends on what we feel its purpose is within the larger argument of the epistle. It is generally held that the heavenly ascent described in 12.2-4 is deliberately inserted into Paul's argument in order to contrast *his* experience with that of his opponents. However, one recent challenge has been mounted against this interpretation. J.D. Tabor (1986) argues that Paul is not trying to win the argument by means of a spiritual one-upmanship, although he is asserting his apostolic authority over the Corinthians through the relation of the extraordinary experience. In Tabor's view, however, the focus of 2 Cor. 12.2-4 is on the heavenly ascent as a foretaste of the ultimate glorification which awaits all believers. In short, Paul uses his experience of 'being caught up to paradise' not so much as an apology, but as a way of expressing his eschatological convictions. Tabor offers an interesting interpretation of what has long been a difficult passage, but it does not do justice to the wider context of 10.7–12.18. Paul builds upon the idea of 'boasting' throughout these chapters, with the claims of his opponents ever present as a foil, a point of contrast. Thus, it is difficult to separate Paul's boast of a heavenly journey from the defence of his apostleship.

Finally, brief mention must be made of A.F. Segal's *Paul the Convert: The Apostolate and Apostasy of Saul the Pharisee* (1990), one of the most creative (and controversial!) interpretations of Paul to be put forward in recent years. With this book Segal boldly enters the arena of scholarly debate over the role that Paul had in the development of Christianity as a religious faith separate and distinct from Judaism. The heavenly journey of 2 Cor. 12.1-10 figures large in Segal's work, helping him establish that Paul was one given over to ecstatic experiences and thus well within the traditions of the mystical-apocalyptic Judaism of his day. He takes the mystical experience of 2 Cor. 12.1-10 to be a true *conversion* of Paul (as opposed to an apostolic *calling or commissioning*) and insists that this experience formed a transition point which influenced the rest of his life and teaching. Paul is thus a *convert* from one form of Judaism to

another, from Pharisaism to Christianity, although (as the
book's sub-title states) he was at the same time viewed by
some of his fellow Jews as an *apostate* from Judaism. For our
considerations here what is most important about this study
is the way in which the visionary experience recorded in
2 Cor. 12.1-10, one among the many that Segal suggests Paul
had, is used in a reconstruction of Paul's life, and beyond
that, in a reconstruction of Jewish–Christian relations in the
first century. Not many agree with all of the details
contained in Segal's work and he has been criticized on
several fronts. Notable among these are his ideas of how the
Mosaic law was viewed by the converted Paul to function in
the lives of Jews and Christians; his rather methodologically
suspect assessment of Pharisaic Judaism; his over-reliance
on Acts in presenting a picture of Paul as an ecstatic figure;
his tendency to overlook the eschatological dimension of
Paul's thought (focusing in the 'vertical' dimension of
visionary experience at the expense of the 'horizontal' dimension of time-which-is-fulfilled); and his modernistic definition
of what constitutes 'conversion'. Nevertheless, Segal presents
us with an intriguing suggestion about the importance of the
mystical experiences of Paul. Far from seeing 2 Cor. 12.1-10
as an isolated, rather eccentric episode in Paul's life, the
interpreter is challenged to see the passage as absolutely
central to an understanding of the apostle's life and ministry.
The heavenly journey motif is thus moved from the wings to
centre stage.

'A Thorn in the Flesh' (12.7)

A variety of interpretations has been suggested as to what
Paul means by the 'thorn in the flesh' with which he had
been afflicted. In the main these interpretations can be
grouped into three categories: those which see the thorn in
the flesh as a physical disability of some sort, such as
malaria, epilepsy, a speech impediment, or chronic eye
trouble; those which see it as a mental, psychological or spiritual condition, a manic-depressive illness, perhaps, or a
tendency to paranoia, or a struggle with sexually impure
thoughts, or extreme anxiety about the fate of his fellow

Jews brought about by their rejection of the gospel; and those
which take it to be a figure of speech used to identify
someone or something external to Paul with whom he had to
contend, a foe. There is something to be said for drawing
attention to the crucifixion of Jesus Christ as lying at the
heart of Paul's statement here. The noun σκόλοψ ('thorn') can
mean 'stake' in the sense of an instrument used 'to stake
(someone) out' or 'to stake (someone) down'. Certainly by the
time of the pagan writer Lucian of Samosata (c. 175 CE) the
crucifixion was being parodied as a 'staking out' of Jesus just
as the tragic figure of Prometheus had been 'staked out' by
the vengeful Zeus. In any case, endless possibilities have
been put forward by commentators over the years as to the
meaning of the 'thorn in the flesh' and there is no reason to
rehearse them all here. However, there are several recent
interpretations which demonstrate how some of the newer
historical-critical tools and insights are being brought to bear
in the interpretative debate; these are of some interest
insofar as they illustrate fresh attempts to solve an old
mystery.

For example, P. Marshall (1987) takes the 'thorn in the
flesh' to be a socially debilitating disease or physical disfigurement which made Paul the object of public ridicule, effectively applying insights from the field of sociology to address
the question. Although Marshall does not say what he thinks
this disease or disfigurement might have been, it is not without significance that he discusses its effects upon Paul
predominantly within the social arena. The most ingenious,
if somewhat speculative, interpretations are those of the
third category. An oft-cited advocate of this classic approach
is T.Y. Mullins (1957) who took the 'thorn in the flesh' to
refer to a particular opponent of Paul whose opposition was
sharp and telling, a person who was the cause of some humil-
iation for the apostle. Central to Mullins's case are the
frequent instances in the Old Testament where Israel's
enemies are described in terms of them being 'thorns' in the
side of the people of God (as in Num. 33.55 and Ezek. 28.24).
M.L. Barré (1980) follows this line of approach, associating
the 'thorn in the flesh' with the idea of weakness which
frames the passage under discussion (see 11.29 and 12.10).

Barré's novel way of supporting this interpretation is to call
attention to parallel ideas from select Qumran texts in which
'weakness' was a metaphor of persecution from one's
enemies. Here we see extra-biblical material being called into
service as an explanation of the Pauline image. Another
similar interpretation is that of R.M. Price (1980), who takes
the image of the 'thorn in the flesh' to be intimately linked to
the passage in which it is set, namely the relation of a heavenly journey by Paul (12.1-6). He suggests that within the
heavenly vision Paul was subjected to a severe buffeting by
an angelic being as part of a punishment for his excessive
pride over having the visionary experience. Crucial to this
interpretation of the image of the 'thorn in the flesh' is the
background of Jewish writings in the tradition of *merkabah*
mysticism (discussed above). R.M. Price's suggestion that the
'thorn in the flesh' passage (12.7-10) should be seen as closely
related to the heavenly journey passage (12.1-6) is taken up
and modified slightly by J.-P. Ruiz (1994). Here, however, the
whole pericope of 12.1-10 is compared with another heavenly
vision, namely Revelation 10. Ruiz suggests that the two
texts, when juxtaposed, demonstrate many remarkable similarities in structure and imagery. More to the point, the
'thorn in the flesh' image in 2 Cor. 12.7 has as its counterpart
the 'eating of the scroll' image in Rev. 10.4. Just as Paul is
given the bodily 'thorn' so that he might be able to proclaim
the power of the gospel even in the midst of weakness, so is
the seer of the Apocalypse given a 'scroll' to ingest bodily,
even though it is bitter. The prophetic calling of both Paul
and the Seer (the author of Revelation) is asserted by means
of these provocative, if puzzling, images.

It is noteworthy that what unites these last four interpretations of Paul's 'thorn in the flesh' is the appeal to external,
secondary sources from Judaism or Christianity as providing
a clue for our understanding of this mysterious image.

Finally, one other recent interpretation of Paul's 'thorn in
the flesh' needs also to be mentioned—that of J.W. McCant
(1988) which rightly approaches the question from the standpoint of how it reflects the debate over Paul's role as an
apostle amongst the Corinthians. The suggestion here is that
the enigmatic phrase is actually a metaphor for the

Corinthian church itself in that it refuses to acknowledge the legitimacy of Paul's apostleship. As McCant puts it (pp. 570-71):

Paul is in a life-and-death struggle over what it means to be a true apostle. Thus he parodies his relationship with the Corinthians as a 'sickness'; because he has not produced 'evidence' that he is a θεῖος ἀνήρ, he has been rejected as an apostle. This rejection of his apostolate at Corinth is thus depicted as a 'sickness'...The 'thorn' is symbolic of Corinth's rejection of Paul's apostolate.

What is to be noted here is the way in which rhetorical-critical analyses of Paul's letters are applied to the interpretation of this most puzzling of images.

Suggestions for Further Reading

On 'The Affliction in Asia' (2 Cor. 1.8-10)
C. Kruse, 'The Price Paid for a Ministry among Gentiles: Paul's Persecution at the Hands of the Jews', in M.J. Wilkins and T. Paige (eds.), *Worship, Theology and Ministry in the Early Church: Essays in Honor of Ralph P. Martin* (JSNTSup, 87; Sheffield: JSOT Press, 1992), pp. 260-72.
L.J. Kreitzer, 'A Numismatic Clue to Acts 19.23-41. The Ephesian Cistophori of Claudius and Agrippina', *JSNT* 30 (1987), pp. 59-70.
R. Yates, 'Paul's Affliction in Asia: 2 Corinthians 1.8', *EvQ* 51 (1983), pp. 241- 45.

On 'Led Forth in Triumph' (2 Cor. 2.14)
V. Bartling, 'God's Triumphant Captive: Christ's Aroma for God (2 Cor. 2.12-17)', *CTM* 22 (1951), pp. 883-94.
P.B. Duff, 'Metaphor, Motif, and Meaning: The Rhetorical Strategy behind the Image "Led in Triumph" in 2 Corinthians 2.14', *CBQ* 53 (1991), pp. 79-92.
R.B. Egan, 'Lexical Evidence on Two Pauline Passages', *NovT* 19 (1977), pp. 34-62.
T.W. Manson, '2 Cor. 2.14-17. Suggestions toward an Exegesis', in J.N. Sevester and W.C. Van Unnik (eds.), *Studia Paulina: In Honour of Johannis De Zwaan* (Haarlem: Bohn, 1953), pp. 155-62.
P. Marshall, 'A Metaphor of Social Shame: *Thriambeuein* in 2 Cor. 2.14', *NovT* 25 (1983), pp. 302-17.
J.I.H. McDonald, 'Paul and the Preaching Ministry: A Reconsideration of 2 Cor. 2.14-17 in its Context', *JSNT* 17 (1983), pp. 35-50.
L. Williamson, 'Led in Triumph: Paul's Use of *Thriambeuo*', *Int* 22 (1968), pp. 317-32.

On 'The Lord Is the Spirit' (3.17)
J.D.G. Dunn, '2 Corinthians III.17—"The Lord Is the Spirit" ', *JTS* 21 (1970), pp. 309-20.

On 'Embodying Death in the Midst of Life' (4.10-12)

P.B. Duff, 'Apostolic Suffering and the Language of Processions in 2 Corinthians 4.7-10', *BTB* 21 (1991), pp. 158-65.

J. Lambrecht, 'The Nekrosis of Jesus: Ministry and Suffering in 2 Cor. 4.7-12', in A. Vanhoye (ed.), *L'Apôtre Paul: Personnalité, style et conception du ministère* (Leuven: Leuven University Press, 1986), pp. 120-43.

C.M. Proudfoot, 'Imitation or Realistic Participation?', *Int* 17 (1963), pp. 140-60.

R.C. Tannehill, *Dying and Rising with Christ: A Study in Pauline Theology* (BZNW, 32; Berlin: Töpelmann, 1967), pp. 84-90.

C. Wolff, 'Humility and Self-Denial in Jesus' Life and Message and in the Apostolic Existence of Paul', in A.J.M. Wedderburn (ed.), *Paul and Jesus: Collected Essays* (JSNTSup, 37; Sheffield: JSOT Press, 1989), pp. 145-60.

On 'Destruction of the Earthly Tent' (5.1-10)

E.E. Ellis, 'The Structure of Pauline Eschatology (II Corinthians v:1-10)', *NTS* 6 (1959–60), pp. 211-24.

J. Gillman, 'A Thematic Comparison: 1 Cor. 15.50-57 and 2 Cor. 5.1-5', *JBL* 107 (1988), pp. 439-54.

M.J. Harris, '2 Corinthians 5.1-10. Watershed in Paul's Eschatology?', *TynBul* 22 (1971), pp. 32-57.

L.J. Kreitzer, *Jesus and God in Paul's Eschatology* (JSNTSup, 19; Sheffield: JSOT Press, 1987).

—'Intermediate State', in G.F. Hawthorne, R.P. Martin and D.G. Reid (eds.), *Dictionary of Paul and his Letters* (Leicester: Inter-Varsity Press, 1993), pp. 438-41.

J. Murphy-O'Connor, ' "Being at Home in the Body we are in Exile from the Lord" ', *RB* 93 (1986), pp. 214-21.

—'Faith and Resurrection in 2 Cor. 4.13-14', *RB* 95 (1988), pp. 543-50.

B. Myer, 'Did Paul's View of the Resurrection of the Dead Undergo Development?', *TS* 47 (1986), pp. 363-87.

J. Osei-Bonsu, 'Does 2 Cor. 5.1-10 Teach the Reception of the Resurrection Body at the Moment of Death?', *JSNT* 28 (1986), pp. 81-101.

C.M. Pate, *Adam Christology as the Exegetical and Theological Substructure of 2 Corinthians 4.7–5.21* (Lanham, MD: University Press of America, 1991).

A.C. Perriman, 'Paul and the Parousia: 1 Corinthians 15.50-57 and 2 Corinthians 5.1-5', *NTS* 35 (1989), pp. 512-21.

J.P.M. Sweet, 'A House not Made with Hands', in W. Horbury (ed.), *Templum Amicitiae: Essays on the Second Temple Presented to Ernst Bammel* (JSNTSup, 48; Sheffield: JSOT Press, 1991), pp. 368-90.

M.E. Thrall, ' "Putting on" or "Stripping off" in 2 Cor. 5.3', in E.J. Epp and G.D. Fee (eds.), *New Testament Textual Criticism: Essays in Honour of Bruce M. Metzger* (Oxford: Clarendon Press, 1981), pp. 221-37.

On 'Knowing Christ According to the Flesh' (5.16)

F.F. Bruce, 'Paul and the Historical Jesus', *BJRL* 56 (1973–74), pp. 321-35.

R. Bultmann, *Primitive Christianity in its Contemporary Setting* (New York: Word Publishing, 1956).

—*Faith and Understanding*, I (London: SCM Press, 1966), pp. 220-246.

F.W. Danker, 'The Theology of 2 Corinthians 5.14-21', in J.P. Lewis (ed.), *Interpreting 2 Corinthians 5.14-21: An Exercise in Hermeneutics* (SBEC, 17; Queenston, Ontario: Edwin Mellen Press, 1989), pp. 87-102.

J.W. Fraser, 'Paul's Knowledge of Jesus: II Corinthians 5.16 Once More', *NTS* 17 (1971), pp. 293-313.

J.L. Martyn, 'Epistemology at the Turn of the Ages: 2 Corinthians 5.16', in W.R. Farmer, C.F.D. Moule and R.R. Niebuhr (eds.), *Christian History and Interpretation: Studies Presented to John Knox* (Cambridge: Cambridge University Press, 1967), pp. 269-87.

C.F.D. Moule, 'Jesus in New Testament Kerygma', in O. Böcher and K. Haacker (eds.), *Verborum Veritas: Festschrift für Gustav Stählin zum 70.Geburtstag* (Wuppertal: Theologischer Verlag Rolf Brockhaus, 1970), pp. 15-26.

J. O'Neill, 'The Absence of the "in Christ" Theology in 2 Corinthians 5', *ABR* 35 (1987), pp. 99-106.

D.W. Oostendorp, *Another Jesus: A Gospel of Jewish-Christian Superiority in II Corinthians* (Kampen: J.H. Kok, 1967).

F.C. Porter, 'Does Paul Claim to Have Known the Historical Jesus? A Study of 2 Corinthians 5.16', *JBL* 47 (1928), pp. 257-75.

G.N. Stanton, *Jesus of Nazareth in New Testament Preaching* (SNTSMS, 27; Cambridge: Cambridge University Press, 1974), pp. 86-116.

C. Wolff, 'True Apostolic Knowledge of Christ: Exegetical Reflections on 2 Corinthians 5.14ff', in A.J.M. Wedderburn (ed.), *Paul and Jesus: Collected Essays* (JSNTSup, 37; Sheffield: JSOT Press, 1989), pp. 81-98.

On 'He Who Knew No Sin' (5.21)

C.B. Cousar, 'II Corinthians 5.17-21', *Int* 35 (1981), pp. 180-83.

F.W. Danker, 'The Theology of 2 Corinthians 5.14-21', in J.P. Lewis (ed.), *Interpreting 2 Corinthians 5.14-21: An Exercise in Hermeneutics* (SBEC, 17; Queenston, Ontario: Edwin Mellen Press, 1989), pp. 87-102.

R.E. Davies, 'Christ in our Place—the Contribution of the Prepositions', *TB* 21 (1970), pp. 71-91.

J.D.G. Dunn, 'Paul's Understanding of the Death of Jesus', in R. Banks (ed.), *Reconciliation and Hope: New Testament Essays on Atonement and Eschatology Presented to L.L. Morris on his 60th Birthday* (Exeter: Paternoster Press, 1974), pp. 125-41.

P. Ellingworth, ' "For our Sake God Made him Share our Sin"? (2 Corinthians 5.21, GNB)', *BT* 38 (1987), pp. 237-41.

J.A. Fitzmyer, 'Reconciliation in Pauline Theology', in J.W. Flanagan and A.W. Robinson (eds.), *No Famine in the Land: Studies in Honor of John L. Mackenzie* (Missoula, MT: Scholars Press, 1975), pp. 155-77. [Reprinted in *To Advance the Gospel* (New York: Crossroad, 1981), pp. 162-85.]

M.J. Harris, 'Appendix: Prepositions and Theology in the Greek New Testament', *NIDNTT*, III, pp. 1171-215.

E. Käsemann, 'Some Thoughts on the Theme "The Doctrine of Reconciliation in the New Testament" ', in J.M. Robinson (ed.), *The Future of our Religious Past* (London: SCM Press, 1971), pp. 49-64.

J. Koenig, 'The Knowing of Glory and its Consequences (2 Corinthians 3–5)', in R.T. Fortna and B.R. Gaventa (eds.), *The Conversation Continues: Studies in Paul and John in Honor of J. Louis Martyn* (Nashville: Abingdon Press, 1990), pp. 158-69.

I.H. Marshall, 'The Meaning of "Reconciliation" ', in R.A. Guelich (ed.), *Unity and Diversity in New Testament Theology: Essays in Honor of George E. Ladd* (Grand Rapids: Eerdmans, 1978), pp. 117-32. [Reprinted in *Jesus the Saviour: Studies in New Testament Theology* (London: SPCK, 1990), pp. 258-74.]

R.P. Martin, *Reconciliation: A Study of Paul's Theology* (London: Marshall, Morgan & Scott, 1981).

S.E. Porter, Καταλλάσσω *in Ancient Greek Literature, with Reference to the Pauline Writings* (EFN, 5; Cordoba: Edicione El Almendro, 1994).

P. Stuhlmacher, *Reconciliation, Law and Righteousness: Essays in Biblical Theology* (Philadelphia: Fortress Press, 1986).

M.E. Thrall, 'Salvation Proclaimed: Part 5. 2 Corinthians 5.18-21', *ExpTim* 93 (1981–82), pp. 227-32.

D.E.H. Whiteley, 'St Paul's Thought on the Atonement', *JTS* 8 (1957), pp. 240-55.

N.T. Wright, 'On Becoming the Righteousness of God: 2 Corinthians 5.21', in D.M. Hay (ed.), *Pauline Theology. II. 1 & 2 Corinthians* (Minneapolis: Fortress Press, 1993), pp. 200-208.

On 'The One who Did the Wrong' (7.12)

C. Kruse, 'The Offender and the Offence in 2 Corinthians 2.5 and 7.12', *EvQ* 60 (1988), pp. 129-39.

—'The Relationship between the Opposition to Paul Reflected in 2 Corinthians 1–7 and 10–13', *EvQ* 61 (1989), pp. 195-202.

M.E. Thrall, 'The Offender and the Offence: A Problem of Detection in 2 Corinthians', in B.P. Thompson (ed.), *Scripture: Meaning and Method: Essays Presented to Anthony Tyrrell Hanson* (Hull: Hull University Press, 1987), pp. 65-78.

On 'Caught up to the Third Heaven' (12.2)

W. Baird, 'Visions, Revelation, and Ministry: Reflections on 2 Cor. 12.1-5 and Gal. 1.11-17', *JBL* 104 (1985), pp. 651-62.

J.W. Bowker, ' "Merkabah" Visions and the Visions of Paul', *JJS* 16 (1971), pp. 157-73.

A.T. Lincoln, ' "Paul the Visionary": The Setting and Significance of the Rapture to Paradise in II Corinthians XII. 1-10', *NTS* 25 (1979), pp. 204-20.

C.R.A. Murray-Jones, 'Paradise Revisited (2 Cor. 12.1-12): The Jewish Background of Paul's Apostolate', *HTR* 86 (1993), pp. 177-217 and 265-93.

P. Schäfer, 'New Testament and Hekalot Literature: The Journey into Heaven in Paul and in Merkavah Mysticism', *JJS* 35 (1984), pp. 19-35.

A.F. Segal, 'Paul and Ecstasy', in K.H. Richards (ed), *Society of Biblical Literature Seminar Papers* (Atlanta: Scholars Press, 1986), pp. 555-80.

—*Paul the Convert: The Apostolate and Apostasy of Saul the Pharisee* (London: Yale University Press, 1990).

R.P. Spittler, 'The Limits of Ecstasy: An Exegesis of 2 Corinthians 12.1-10', in G.F. Hawthorne (ed.), *Current Issues in Biblical and Patristic Interpretation: Studies in Honor of Merrill C. Tenney* (Grand Rapids, MI: Eerdmans, 1975), pp. 259-66.

J.D. Tabor, *Things Unutterable: Paul's Ascent to Paradise in its Greco-Roman, Judaic, and Early Christian Contexts* (SJ; Lanham, MD: University Press of America, 1986).

On *'A Thorn in the Flesh' (12.7)*

M.L. Barré, 'Qumran and the Weakness of Paul', *CBQ* 42 (1980), pp. 216-27.

J.W. McCant, 'Paul's Thorn of Rejected Apostleship', *NTS* 34 (1988), pp. 550-72.

P.H. Menoud, 'The Thorn in the Flesh and Satan's Angel (2 Cor. 12.7)', in *Jesus Christ and the Faith: A Collection of Studies* (Pittsburgh: Pickwick, 1978), pp.19-30.

T.Y. Mullins, 'Paul's Thorn in the Flesh', *JBL* 76 (1957), pp. 299-303.

D.M. Park, 'Paul's ΣΚΟΛΟΨ ΤΗ ΣΑΡΚΙ: Thorn or Stake? (2 Cor. XII 7)', *NovT* 22 (1980), pp. 179-83.

R.M. Price, 'Punished in Paradise: An Exegetical Theory on II Corinthians 12.1-10', *JSNT* 7 (1980), pp. 33-40.

J.-P. Ruiz, 'Hearing and Seeing but not Saying: A Look at Revelation 10.4 and 2 Corinthians 12.4', in E.H. Lovering, Jr (ed.), *Society of Biblical Literature Seminar Papers* (Atlanta: Scholars Press, 1994), pp. 182-202.

8

THE CHALLENGE OF 2 CORINTHIANS FOR THE MODERN WORLD

THERE ARE SEVERAL WAYS in which 2 Corinthians challenges the modern reader, particularly as we fast approach the end of the millennium. Here I would like briefly to outline four which may prove to be among the most relevant in the years to come. I simply offer them as opportunities for further thought and reflection on how this most enigmatic of Paul's epistles will continue to guide and shape our thinking.

First, there is the challenge which the epistle presents to the world of biblical scholarship. The essential point here is that no matter how advanced we may feel critical scholarship to be, 2 Corinthians seems to defy complete explanation. In short, the letter challenges the confidence of scholars who think that the New Testament can ever be fully fathomed, that we can ever plumb the depths of Scripture. Not all of the questions we would like to pose can ever be answered. In this sense 2 Corinthians is (to borrow a phrase from Sir Winston Churchill) 'a riddle wrapped in a mystery, inside an enigma'. Exactly how many letters are actually contained within our canonical 2 Corinthians, and the precise nature of the historical and theological relationships between them, are matters about which we shall never be able to decide with any degree of certainty. At best we can make educated guesses, professional hunches, about such matters, but nothing more than that. At times this has proven to be a very humbling experience for scholars who all too easily deceive themselves into believing that the historical-critical method can solve every problem, provided that it is given enough time and information. Such self-confidence is misplaced when we move to consider 2 Corinthians, and can even appear to be arrogant. In short, there is a note of humility here which needs to be remembered.

Secondly, 2 Corinthians offers a challenge to the prosperity gospel which is so characteristic of large sections of our late twentieth-century Western society. Far from offering a message of unending bliss, and a promise of a Christian life which is without difficulties, 2 Corinthians brutally asserts that suffering is an essential part of the Christian message and that it has been so from the beginning. Nothing challenges the credibility of the Christian cause more powerfully in many parts of the world than the casual assumption that material and financial blessing is part and parcel of God's approval and acceptance. Within 2 Corinthians Paul continually addresses this issue, stressing how God's power is manifested in human weakness, how physical poverty is really to be seen as spiritual wealth, how personal inability is transformed into divine opportunity. Nowhere else in the Pauline corpus is the truth of Ernest Hemingway's provocative phrase from *A Farewell to Arms* (1929) that 'we are strong in the broken places' made more clear. Paul's whole apostolic ministry, so much a central issue in 2 Corinthians, is illustrative of this point.

Thirdly, 2 Corinthians presents us with a challenge to inter-faith relationships, particularly those between Jews and Christians. I had occasion to note above that over the years a large amount of attention has been given to identifying Paul's opposition in Corinth. One common assumption in this matter is that Jewish opponents are at the centre of the controversy, and this has helped set the stage for tensions between Jewish and Christian interpreters of Paul's life and letters. However, this assumption that Paul's opponents in Corinth were Jewish Christians who were trying to impose a Torah-based lifestyle upon the Gentile Christians is widely questioned today. Surely it is not without significance that the movement in recent years away from seeing Judaizers as responsible for the problems in Corinth comes at the same time as there has been a marked improvement in Jewish–Christian relationships, particularly among scholars from both faith communities. One wonders how much of our interpretation of Paul continues to be governed by questionable assumptions about how Jewish Christians and Gentile Christians perceived their living together.

Fourthly, following the challenge that 2 Corinthians presents in terms of inter-faith dialogue, note also the challenge which the letter presents on the ecumenical scene within the Christian church as a whole. Not only can Paul's advice and teaching here be usefully applied to individual congregations and to local fellowships, but so too can many of the truths about learning to live together be usefully applied to many of the denominational and ecclesiastical battles which so characterize our day. The challenge for Christians to learn to live in peace with one another is a very real one, and may prove to be one of the most difficult to address. Perhaps we need to take a leaf from Paul's book and focus on a modern-day equivalent to the Jerusalem collection so as to forge inter-church cooperation and a sense of common commitment to a larger cause. Could not the threat of genocide in Africa, whether it is due to famine, or civil war, or short-sighted development policies, or a combination of all of these, provide just such a focus of concern? Or perhaps the threat of AIDS, wiping out a whole generation of people in some parts of the world and making any hope for the future non-existent for those who remain, could be a focal point? These are difficult issues to solve, but I cannot help but wonder if tackling them is to follow in the true spirit of Christianity as Paul understood it. Thus, it may well be that only when challenges such as these are honestly faced can the words with which Paul ends the letter, regularly spoken by congregations around the world as a confession of faith, become true:

> May the grace of our Lord Jesus Christ, the love of God, and the fellowship of the Holy Spirit be with us all. Amen!

Commentaries and Studies on 2 Corinthians

Commentaries Requiring Knowledge of Greek
C.K. Barrett, *The Second Epistle to the Corinthians* (BNTC; London: A. & C. Black, 1973).
H.D. Betz, *2 Corinthians 8 and 9: A Commentary on Two Administrative Letters of Paul* (Hermeneia; Philadelphia: Fortress Press, 1985).
R. Bultmann, *The Second Letter to the Corinthians* (Minneapolis: Augsburg, 1985). [Based on a handwritten manuscript written between 1940–1952 and first published in German in 1976.]
V.P. Furnish, *II Corinthians* (AB, 32a; Garden City, NY: Doubleday, 1984).
J. Héring, *The Second Epistle of Saint Paul to the Corinthians* (London: Epworth Press, 1967).
R.P. Martin, *2 Corinthians* (WBC, 40; Waco, TX: Word Books, 1986).
C.H. Talbert, *Reading Corinthians: A Literary and Theological Commentary on 1 and 2 Corinthians* (New York: Crossroad, 1987).
M.E. Thrall, *The Second Epistle to the Corinthians 1–7* (ICC; Edinburgh: T. & T. Clark, 1994).
H. Windisch, *Der zweite Korintherbrief* (MeyerK, 6; Göttingen: Vandenhoeck & Ruprecht, 1924).

Commentaries not Requiring Detailed Knowledge of Greek
W. Baird, *1 Corinthians/2 Corinthians* (KPG; Atlanta: John Knox Press, 1980).
P.W. Barnett, *The Message of 2 Corinthians* (BST; Leicester: Inter-Varsity Press, 1988).
G.R. Beasley-Murray, *2 Corinthians* (BBC, 11; Nashville: Broadman Press, 1971), pp. 1-76.
E. Best, *Second Corinthians* (IC; Atlanta: John Knox Press, 1987).
F.F. Bruce, *1 and 2 Corinthians* (NCB; London: Marshall, Morgan & Scott, 1971).
D.A. Carson, *From Triumphalism to Maturity: A New Exposition of 2 Corinthians 10–13* (Leicester: Inter-Varsity Press, 1984).
F.W. Danker, *II Corinthians* (AC; Minneapolis: Augsburg, 1989).
M.J. Harris, *2 Corinthians* (EBC, 10; Grand Rapids: Zondervan, 1976), pp. 299-406.
P.E. Hughes, *Paul's Second Epistle to the Corinthians* (NICNT; Grand Rapids: Eerdmans, 1962).
C. Kruse, *2 Corinthians* (TNTC; Leicester: Inter-Varsity Press, 1987).
N. Watson, *The Second Epistle to the Corinthians* (EC; London: Epworth Press, 1993).

Dictionary Articles and Contributions in One-Volume Works

H.D. Betz, 'Corinthians, Second Epistle to the', *ABD*, I, pp. 1148-54.

D. Georgi, 'Corinthians, Second', *IDBSup*, pp. 183-86.

S.J. Hafemann, 'Corinthians, Letters to the', in G.F. Hawthorne, R.P. Martin and D.G. Reid (eds.), *Dictionary of Paul and his Letters* (Leicester: Inter-Varsity Press, 1993), pp. 164-79.

C. Hickling, 'Corinthian Correspondence', in R.J. Coggins and J.L. Houlden (eds.), *A Dictionary of Biblical Interpretation* (London: SCM Press, 1990), pp. 139-42.

J. Murphy-O'Connor, 'The Second Letter to the Corinthians', in R.E. Brown, J.A. Fitzmyer and R.E. Murphy (eds.), *The New Jerome Biblical Commentary* (London: Geofffrey Chapman, 1991), pp. 816-29.

C.S.C. Williams, 'I & II Corinthians', in M. Black and H.H. Rowley (eds.), *Peake's Commentary on the Bible* (Sunbury-on-Thames: Thomas Nelson, 1962), pp. 954-72.

Specialized Studies on Paul and on the Corinthian Epistles

C.K. Barrett, *Essays on Paul* (London: SPCK, 1982).

—*Paul: An Introduction to his Thought* (London: Geoffrey Chapman, 1994).

K. Barth, *The Epistle to the Romans* (Oxford: Oxford University Press, 1993).

E. Best, *Paul and his Converts* (Edinburgh: T. & T. Clark, 1988).

G. Bornkamm, *Paul* (London: Hodder & Stoughton, 1971).

F.F. Bruce, *Paul: Apostle of the Heart Set Free* (Grand Rapids: Eerdmans, 1977).

J.-F. Collange, *Enigmes de la deuxième épître de Paul aux Corinthiens: Etude exegetique de 2 Cor. 2,14–7,4* (SNTSMS, 18: Cambridge: Cambridge University Press, 1972).

J.A. Crafton, *The Agency of the Apostle: A Dramatic Analysis of Paul's Responses to Conflict in 2 Corinthians* (JSNTSup, 51; Sheffield: JSOT Press, 1991).

N.A. Dahl, *Studies in Paul: Theology for the Early Christian Mission* (Minneapolis: Augsburg, 1977).

M. Dibelius and W.G. Kümmel, *Paul* (London: Longmans, Green & Co., 1953).

G.D. Fee, *God's Empowering Presence: The Holy Spirit in the Letters of Paul* (Peabody, MA: Hendrickson, 1994).

D. Georgi, *Remembering the Poor: The History of Paul's Collection for Jerusalem* (Nashville: Abingdon Press, 1992 [1965]).

S.J. Hafemann, *Suffering and Ministry in the Spirit: Paul's Defense of his Ministry in II Cor. 2.14–3.3* (Grand Rapids: Eerdmans, 1990).

—*Paul, Moses and the History of Israel: The Letter/Spirit Contrast and the Argument from Scripture in 2 Corinthians 3* (WUNT, 81; Tübingen: Mohr [Paul Siebeck], 1995).

A.T. Hanson, *Studies in Paul's Technique and Theology* (London: SPCK, 1974).

—*Paradox in the Thought of St Paul* (JSNTSup, 17; Sheffield: JSOT Press, 1987).

M.J. Harris, *Raised Immortal: Resurrection and Immortality in New Testament Teaching* (London: Marshall, Morgan & Scott, 1983).

R.B. Hays, *Echoes of Scripture in the Letters of Paul* (London: Yale University Press, 1989).

B. Holmberg, *Paul and Power: The Structure of Authority in the Primitive Church as Reflected in the Pauline Epistles* (Philadelphia: Fortress Press, 1978).

M. Hooker, *From Adam to Christ: Essays on Paul* (Cambridge: Cambridge University Press, 1990).

E. Käsemann, 'Die Legitimität des Apostels: Eine Untersuchung zu 2 Korinther 10–13', *ZNW* 41 (1942), pp. 33-71.

—*Perspectives on Paul* (London: SCM Press, 1971), pp. 138-66.

S. Kim, *The Origin of Paul's Gospel* (Grand Rapids: Eerdmans, 1981).

A.T. Lincoln, *Paradise now and not yet: Studies in the Role of the Heavenly Dimension in Paul's Thought with Special Reference to his Eschatology* (SNTSMS, 43; Cambridge: Cambridge University Press, 1981), pp. 55-86.

G. Lüdemann, *Paul, Apostle to the Gentiles: Studies in Chronology* (London: SCM Press, 1984).

—*Opposition to Paul in Jewish Christianity* (Minneapolis: Fortress Press, 1989).

T.W. Manson, 'The Corinthian Correspondence', in M. Black (ed.), *Studies in the Gospels and Epistles* (Manchester: Manchester University Press, 1962), pp. 190-224.

—*On Paul and John* (SBT, 38; London: SCM Press, 1963).

P. Marshall, *Enmity in Corinth: Social Conventions in Paul's Relations with the Corinthians* (WUNT, 2.23; Tübingen: Mohr, 1987).

W.A. Meeks, *The First Urban Christians: The Social World of the Apostle Paul* (London: Yale University Press, 1983).

J. Murphy-O'Connor, *The Theology of the Second Letter to the Corinthians* (NTTS; Cambridge: Cambridge University Press, 1991).

C.C. Newman, *Paul's Glory-Christology: Tradition and Rhetoric* (NovTSup, 69; Leiden: Brill, 1992).

C.M. Pate, *Adam Christology as the Exegetical and Theological Substructure of 2 Corinthians 4.7–5.21* (Lanham, MD: University Press of America, 1991).

K. Quast, *Reading the Corinthian Correspondence: An Introduction* (Mahwah, NJ: Paulist Press, 1994).

C.J. Roetzel, *The Letters of Paul: Conversations in Context* (London: SCM Press 1983).

E.P. Sanders, *Paul* (Oxford Past Masters; Oxford: Oxford University Press, 1991).

W. Schmithals, *Gnosticism in Corinth: An Investigation of the Letters to the Corinthians* (Nashville: Abingdon Press, 1971).

J.H. Schütz, *Paul and the Anatomy of Apostolic Authority* (SNTSMS, 26; Cambridge: Cambridge University Press, 1975).

J.L. Sumney, *Identifying Paul's Opponents: The Question of Method in 2 Corinthians* (JSNTSup, 66; Sheffield: JSOT Press, 1992).

G. Theissen, *The Social Setting of Pauline Christianity* (Edinburgh: T.& T. Clark, 1982).

F. Watson, '2 Cor. X–XIII and Paul's Painful Letter to the Corinthians', *JTS* 35 (1984), pp. 324-46.

—*Paul, Judaism and the Gentiles: A Sociological Approach* (SNTSMS, 56; Cambridge: Cambridge University Press, 1986).

D. Wenham, *Paul: Follower of Jesus or Founder of Christianity?* (Grand Rapids: Eerdmans, 1995).

F. Young and D.F. Ford, *Meaning and Truth in 2 Corinthians* (BFT; London: SPCK, 1987).

J. Ziesler, *Pauline Christianity* (Oxford: Oxford University Press, rev. edn, 1990).

INDEXES

INDEX OF REFERENCES

OLD TESTAMENT

OTHER ANCIENT REFERENCES

INDEX OF AUTHORS

Tannehill, R.C.   102, 128
Taylor, N.H.   37, 87
Theissen, G.   46, 47, 138
Thrall, M.E.   12, 26, 27, 37, 54, 76, 82,
   119, 120, 128, 130, 135
Tidball, D.   54
Travis, S.H.   55

Van Unnik, W.C.   59, 70

Walker, W.O.   92
Watson, F.   20, 41, 47, 80, 81, 138
Watson, N.   12, 135
Webb, W.J.   34, 37
Weber, M.   46
Welborn, L.L.   37

Wenham, D.   18, 54, 138
Westerholm, S.   70
Whiteley, D.E.H.   113, 130
Williams, C.S.C.   136
Williamson, L.   96, 127
Windisch, H.   28, 135
Witherington, B.   53, 55, 68, 70
Wolff, C.   128, 129
Wright, N.T.   64, 70, 130

Yates, R.   94, 127
Young, F.   48, 49, 138

Ziesler, J.   12, 138
Zmijewski, J.   55